# Oracle Database XE 11gR2 Jump Start Guide

Build and manage your Oracle Database 11g XE environment with this fast paced, practical guide

**Asif Momen**

BIRMINGHAM - MUMBAI

# Oracle Database XE 11gR2 Jump Start Guide

First published: July 2012

Production Reference: 1290612

Published by Packt Publishing Ltd.
Livery Place
35 Livery Street
Birmingham B3 2PB, UK.

ISBN 978-1-84968-674-7

www.packtpub.com

Cover Image by Mark Holland (MJH767@bham.ac.uk)

# Credits

**Author**
Asif Momen

**Reviewers**
Satishbabu Gunukula
Edgar Lanting
Marcin Przepiórowski
Carol A. Pena

**Acquisition Editor**
Dhwani Devater

**Lead Technical Editor**
Dayan Hyames

**Technical Editors**
Vrinda Amberkar
Devdutt Kulkarni
Prashant Salvi

**Project Coordinator**
Yashodhan Dere

**Proofreader**
Aaron Nash

**Indexer**
Rekha Nair

**Graphics**
Manu Joseph

**Production Coordinators**
Prachali Bhiwandkar
Shantanu Zagade

**Cover Work**
Shantanu Zagade

# About the Author

**Asif Momen** has been working with Oracle Technologies for over 12 years and has expertise in Database Architecture, Performance Tuning, and High Availability. He has a Master's degree in Software Systems from Birla Institute of Technology and Science (BITS), Pilani.

Asif has been honored with the prestigious Oracle ACE award from Oracle Technology Network. He has the OCP 11*g* DBA and OCP 9*i* Forms Developer certifications and is an Oracle Certified Expert in RAC 10*g*.

Asif is a presenter for conferences such as Oracle OpenWorld-2010, All India Oracle User Group (AIOUG), and Brain Surface. In addition to this, he is a member of the Editorial Board for "Oracle Connect", the quarterly publication of AIOUG and the "Select" magazine of the United Kingdom Oracle User Group (UKOUG)

His articles have also appeared in Oracle Support – Customer Knowledge Exchange. His particular interests are Database and SQL tuning, Oracle RAC, and Backup and Recovery. He posts his ideas and opinions on "The Momen Blog" (`http://momendba.blogspot.com`). Asif can be reached at `asif.momen@gmail.com`.

# Acknowledgement

First and foremost, I would like to thank God for giving me the power to believe in my passion and pursue my dreams. I could never have done this without the faith I have in you, the Almighty.

To my parents, Masood and Naseem, for what I am today. I can barely find the right words to express all the wisdom, love, and support you have given me. I cannot forget the sacrifices and hardships you both have gone through just to see me smiling. You are the best parents one could wish for.

To my wonderful wife, Nazia. Your patient love enabled me to complete this work. You have always been supportive and motivating in continuing me to improve my knowledge and move ahead in my career.

To my daughters, Maria, Nida, and Zoha. You are the best children any dad could hope for—sweet, loving, and fun to be with. It's wonderful to watch you grow.

To my friends. You guys have given me the best support when I really needed it. Your silly jokes made me cheerful when I was down. Thanks for staying in touch even when I ignored you guys for a while and for listening to my boring topics for hours together.

Last but not least, the Packt team, thanks a bunch for all of you involved in the production and printing of this book.

# About the Reviewers

**Satishbabu Gunukula** is an Oracle ACE. He has extensive experience in the Oracle and Microsoft SQL Server database technologies, has held various roles such as Tech Lead, Project Lead, and Project Manager, and specialized in High Availability. He has implemented many business critical RAC and MAA systems for fortune 500, 1000 companies. He has experience on a wide range of products such as Oracle Hyperion, SAP Basis, MySQL, Linux, and Business Apps administration.

Satishbabu has done his Master's degree and he is an Oracle Certified DBA in 8*i*/9*i*/10*g* and Oracle Certified Expert in 10*g* RAC. He has written several articles in technical journals and blogs in the US, and spoken at Oracle-related conferences. He shares his knowledge on his websites — www.oracleracexpert.com and www.sqlserver-expert.com.

**Edgar Lanting** has been an IT pro for over 18 years, starting out as a System Administrator on AS/400, Windows, and Unix. After this he made the move to being a DBA. Edgar is versatile and a very skilled Oracle, Microsoft SQL Server, and MySQL Server DBA, and in combination with his past as a System Administrator this has proven to help him see things from more than one perspective when working in the field. Edgar is also a certified Oracle specialist.

Edgar is currently working as a Database Consultant for Ciber in the Netherlands where he assists companies in managing their database environments. In his spare time he likes to go out photographing birds and nature, and enjoys hiking with his wife and dog.

He is currently reviewing the *iWork for Mac OSX Cookbook* for Packt.

**Marcin Przepiórowski** started his Oracle DBA activities in 2000. For the last nine years he has been working as a Senior Oracle DBA and Consultant for many various customers in Poland and Ireland. He is interested in performance bottlenecks (using end-to-end approaches and all available monitoring possibilities), High Availability solutions (such as Oracle Real Application Cluster and Oracle DataGuard) and Backup and Recovery technology.

Marcin is an Oracle ACE and maintainer of the open source Simulated Active Session History (S-ASH) project. He used to publish posts about Oracle technologies on his blog at http://oracleprof.blogspot.com/ and speaks at conferences in Europe.

# www.PacktPub.com

## Support files, eBooks, discount offers and more

You might want to visit www.PacktPub.com for support files and downloads related to your book.

Did you know that Packt offers eBook versions of every book published, with PDF and ePub files available? You can upgrade to the eBook version at www.PacktPub.com and as a print book customer, you are entitled to a discount on the eBook copy. Get in touch with us at service@packtpub.com for more details.

At www.PacktPub.com, you can also read a collection of free technical articles, sign up for a range of free newsletters and receive exclusive discounts and offers on Packt books and eBooks.

http://PacktLib.PacktPub.com

Do you need instant solutions to your IT questions? PacktLib is Packt's online digital book library. Here, you can access, read and search across Packt's entire library of books.

## Why Subscribe?

- Fully searchable across every book published by Packt
- Copy and paste, print and bookmark content
- On demand and accessible via web browser

## Free Access for Packt account holders

If you have an account with Packt at www.PacktPub.com, you can use this to access PacktLib today and view nine entirely free books. Simply use your login credentials for immediate access.

## Instant Updates on New Packt Books

Get notified! Find out when new books are published by following @PacktEnterprise on Twitter, or the *Packt Enterprise* Facebook page.

# Table of Contents

# Preface

*Oracle Database XE 11gR2 Jump Start Guide* helps you to install, administer, maintain, tune, back up, and upgrade your Oracle Database Express Edition. The book also helps you to build custom database applications using Oracle Application Express.

This book is a fast paced, practical guide including clear examples and screenshots to help you better understand the concepts, and details for building and managing your Oracle Database XE environment.

## What this book covers

*Chapter 1, Database Editions and Oracle Database XE,* provides a brief introduction to the various editions of Oracle database and in particular, Oracle Database 11gR2 Express Edition.

*Chapter 2, Installing and Uninstalling Oracle Database XE,* is about installing and uninstalling Oracle Database XE on Windows and Linux environments.

*Chapter 3, Connecting and Configuring Oracle Database 11g XE,* focuses on Oracle Listener configuration and establishing client connections to the database, followed by Oracle memory management.

*Chapter 4, Accessing Table Data, DML Statements, and Transactions,* talks about SQL Developer, accessing table data, modifying table data, understanding transaction control statements, and the most commonly used SQL functions.

*Chapter 5, Creating and Managing Schema Objects,* deals with creating and managing database objects such as tables, indexes, constraints, views, sequences, and synonyms.

*Chapter 6, Developing Stored Subprograms and Triggers,* brings you the power of PL/SQL. In this chapter, you will learn to build stored procedures, functions, and triggers.

*Chapter 7, Building a Sample Application with Oracle Application Express,* provides a brief introduction to Oracle Application Express (APEX). You will learn how to create rich and responsive applications using Oracle Application Express.

*Chapter 8, Managing Database and Database Storage,* provides background information on Oracle memory management, and explains physical database structure and the Flash Recovery Area.

*Chapter 9, Moving Data between Oracle Databases,* explains how to move data between different Oracle Database XE versions using Oracle's export/import utilities.

*Chapter 10, Upgrading Oracle Database 11g XE to Other Database Editions,* explains in detail how to upgrade Oracle Database Express Edition to other Oracle Database Editions.

*Chapter 11, Backup and Recovery,* provides an insight to Oracle's backup and recovery procedures. Backups are to a database what fire fighters are to a city. In this chapter, you will learn how to protect and recover your database.

*Chapter 12, Tuning Oracle Database 11g XE,* provides a systematic approach to performance tuning, avoiding many of the most common application design and development mistakes and tracing of SQL statements.

*Appendix, Features Available with Oracle Database 11g XE,* lists all the features that are available with Oracle Database 11g Express Edition.

# What you need for this book

The hardware requirements are:

- A laptop/desktop with at least 2 GB memory; 4 GB is recommended

The software requirements are:

- Oracle Database 11g Release 2 Express Edition
- Microsoft Windows 7/XP or Oracle Enterprise Linux (or any other version of Linux)
- A web browser on your host OS

# Who this book is for

This book is intended for beginners who wish to learn Oracle Database administration, without the benefit of formal training.

# Conventions

In this book, you will find a number of styles of text that distinguish between different kinds of information. Here are some examples of these styles, and an explanation of their meaning.

Code words in text are shown as follows: " Navigate to the `Disk1` folder under `c:\temp` and double-click on `setup.exe`. A new window pops up."

A block of code is set as follows:

```
groupadd oinstall
groupadd dba
useradd -g oinstall -G dba,oper,asmadmin oracle
passwd oracle
```

Any command-line input or output is written as follows:

```
# /etc/init.d/oracle-xe start
```

**New terms** and **important words** are shown in bold. Words that you see on the screen, in menus or dialog boxes for example, appear in the text like this: "Click on the **Install** button to continue installing Oracle Database XE".

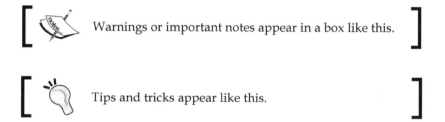

> Warnings or important notes appear in a box like this.

> Tips and tricks appear like this.

# Reader feedback

Feedback from our readers is always welcome. Let us know what you think about this book—what you liked or may have disliked. Reader feedback is important for us to develop titles that you really get the most out of.

To send us general feedback, simply send an e-mail to `feedback@packtpub.com`, and mention the book title through the subject of your message.

If there is a topic that you have expertise in and you are interested in either writing or contributing to a book, see our author guide on `www.packtpub.com/authors`.

# Customer support

Now that you are the proud owner of a Packt book, we have a number of things to help you to get the most from your purchase.

# Downloading the example code

You can download the example code files for all Packt books you have purchased from your account at http://www.packtpub.com. If you purchased this book elsewhere, you can visit http://www.packtpub.com/support and register to have the files e-mailed directly to you.

# Errata

Although we have taken every care to ensure the accuracy of our content, mistakes do happen. If you find a mistake in one of our books—maybe a mistake in the text or the code—we would be grateful if you would report this to us. By doing so, you can save other readers from frustration and help us improve subsequent versions of this book. If you find any errata, please report them by visiting http://www.packtpub.com/support, selecting your book, clicking on the **errata submission form** link, and entering the details of your errata. Once your errata are verified, your submission will be accepted and the errata will be uploaded to our website, or added to any list of existing errata, under the Errata section of that title.

# Piracy

Piracy of copyright material on the Internet is an ongoing problem across all media. At Packt, we take the protection of our copyright and licenses very seriously. If you come across any illegal copies of our works, in any form, on the Internet, please provide us with the location address or website name immediately so that we can pursue a remedy.

Please contact us at copyright@packtpub.com with a link to the suspected pirated material.

We appreciate your help in protecting our authors, and our ability to bring you valuable content.

# Questions

You can contact us at questions@packtpub.com if you are having a problem with any aspect of the book, and we will do our best to address it.

# 1
# Database Editions and Oracle Database XE

*Obstacles are those frightful things you see when you take your eyes off your goal.*
*- Henry Ford*

This chapter briefly introduces various database editions offered by Oracle Database 11*g*, and then introduces Oracle Database XE. We will dive into a list of features supported by Oracle Database XE and also discuss the limitations imposed on Oracle Database XE. The topics that will be covered in this chapter are as follows:

- Available database editions
- Oracle Database Express Edition

## About Oracle

Oracle Corporation is a computer technology company established in 1977. Oracle specializes in developing enterprise software products. Oracle provides database management systems (such as Oracle Database, MySQL, and TimesTen), database development tools (such as Oracle Developer Suite and JDeveloper), **Enterprise Resource Planning (ERP)** software, **Customer Relationship Management (CRM)** software, and so on. With the acquisition of Sun Microsystems, Oracle has emerged as a hardware vendor offering Sun hardware under its umbrella.

In the words of Larry Ellison, the CEO of Oracle, "Oracle will be the only company that can engineer an integrated system—applications to disk—where all the pieces fit and work together so customers do not have to do it themselves. Our customers benefit as their systems integration costs go down while system performance, reliability, and security go up." Read the complete story about "Oracle Buys Sun" at http://www.oracle.com/us/corporate/press/018363.

# Available database editions

Oracle Database 11*g* is available in five editions, namely Enterprise Edition, Standard Edition, Standard Edition One, **Express Edition** (**XE**), and Personal Edition. All editions are built on the same code base. This means we can easily scale up Oracle Express Edition to Standard Edition One to Standard Edition to Enterprise Edition.

To scale up to a higher edition, we would install the new software, open the database in the new edition, run the `catalog.sql` and `catproc.sql` scripts, and recompile the stored procedures. This topic is covered in greater detail later in the book.

- **Personal Edition**: Personal Edition is available on the Windows platform and it supports single-user development environments.

- **Express Edition** (**XE**): XE is a small footprint database. It does not require license from Oracle to develop applications on XE. You can deploy and distribute XE freely without paying a penny as a license fee to Oracle. Database features such as **Automatic Memory Management** (**AMM**), **Advanced Queuing** (**AQ**), Flashback query, and Data Encryption are supported with XE. There are a few limitations on XE, which we will explore later in the chapter. Support is provided through a free Oracle Discussion Forum (`https://forums.oracle.com/forums/forum.jspa?forumID=251&start=0`).

- **Standard Edition One** (**SEO**): SEO is a low cost and full featured database for servers. It provides all database features available with XE and adds a few more to its list. SEO is available on Windows, Linux, and UNIX platforms. As a license fee you pay $900 to Oracle (for five users) and start using SEO. You pay an additional $180 per user if required. The pricing information provided here is subject to change; refer to Oracle's Global Pricing and Licensing for more details (`http://www.oracle.com/us/corporate/pricing/index.html`). Database features such as Java Support, Enterprise Manager and **Automatic Storage Management** (**ASM**) are included in SEO.

- **Standard Edition** (**SE**): SE is an affordable edition of Oracle database. It is a full-featured database for servers up to four sockets. It can easily scale to Enterprise Edition as demand grows. Database features supported by Standard Edition One are supported by SE and it adds few more to its list. **Real Application Clusters** (**RAC**) and **Automatic Workload Management** (**AWM**) are two additional database features supported by Standard Edition.

You pay $1,750 to Oracle towards a license fee, which includes a license for five users. You pay an additional $350 per user if required. It is also compatible with Enterprise Edition and can easily grow with demand. Refer to the Oracle's Global Pricing and Licensing document for more details.

- Enterprise Edition (EE): This edition of Oracle database comes with a range of database options. EE provides industry leading performance, scalability, and security to your database. With Enterprise Edition you get database features such as Total Recall, Active Data Guard, Flashback Database, Real Application Clusters One-Node, Database Vault, Virtual Private Database, and many other that are not found in other database editions. An additional licensing cost is associated with these database features refer to Oracle's Global Pricing and Licensing for more details.

# Oracle Database Express Edition (XE)

Oracle Database XE is an entry level database available on Windows and Linux operating systems. XE is built with the same code base as Oracle Database 11*g* Release 2, so scaling XE to other editions can be easily achieved.

Oracle Database XE is a good starter database for DBAs and developers who need a free database for training and deployment. **Independent Software Vendors** (**ISVs**) and hardware vendors can freely distribute Oracle Database XE along with their products, thus adding value to their own products.

Educational institutions can freely use Oracle Database XE for their curriculum. The following are the features of Oracle Database 11*g* Express Edition:

- Available on Linux (64-bit) and Windows (32-bit)
- Installs using native installers
- Fully upgradeable to other Oracle Database 11*g* editions
- Supports Oracle SQL Developer, Oracle Application Express, Java, .NET and Visual Studio, and PHP development environments

Oracle Database 11*g* Express Edition comes with the following licensing restrictions:

- Executes on one processor in any size server
- Supports up to 11GB of user data
- Uses up to 1GB RAM of available memory in any size server
- Supports one database per machine
- HTTPS is not supported natively with the HTTP listener built into Oracle Database XE

# Summary

At the end of this chapter, you will have a sound understanding of the various database editions available with Oracle Database 11*g*. You will also have a good understanding of the database features available with each database edition.

By now, you will also have an understanding of the features offered by Oracle Database 11*g* XE and also its limitations.

# References

- Oracle Database 11*g* Features comparison by Database Editions (`http://www.oracle.com/us/products/database/product-editions-066501.html`)
- For complete licensing information go to `http://www.oracle.com/us/corporate/pricing/technology-price-list-070617.pdf`

# 2
# Installing and Uninstalling Oracle Database XE

*Though no one can go back and make a brand new start, anyone can start from now and make a brand new ending. - Unknown*

In this chapter we will explore the installation/un-installation of Oracle Database 11*g* XE and starting/stopping the database. Before beginning with the installation, we will look at the system requirements. We will also learn how to start and stop Oracle Database 11*g* XE and finally uninstall it. We will cover both the Windows and Linux environments. This chapter will guide you with the help of screenshots for easy understanding. The topics that will be covered in this chapter are as follows:

- Downloading Oracle Database 11*g* XE
- Installing Oracle Database 11*g* XE on Windows XP (32-bit)
- Starting and stopping Oracle Database XE in Windows
- Uninstalling Oracle Database 11*g* XE on Windows XP (32-bit)
- Installing Oracle Database 11*g* XE on Oracle Enterprise Linux (64-bit)
- Starting and stopping Oracle Database XE in Linux
- Uninstalling Oracle Database 11*g* XE on Oracle Enterprise Linux (64-bit)

# Downloading Oracle Database 11*g* XE

You can download Oracle Database 11*g* XE from Oracle's website (`http://www.oracle.com/technetwork/database/express-edition/downloads/index.html`). To download the software you must sign in to the Oracle website and agree to the license agreement. At the time of writing this book, Oracle Database 11*g* XE is available on the Windows 32-bit and Linux 64-bit platforms. Oracle Database 11*g* XE software is 301 MB and 312 MB in size for Linux and Windows operating systems, respectively. As mentioned earlier, Oracle Database 11*g* XE is a free software.

# Installing Oracle Database 11*g* XE on Windows XP (32-bit)

The installation of Oracle Database 11*g* XE in a Windows environment is pretty straightforward. You can install Oracle Database XE on Microsoft Windows 7, Microsoft Windows Server 2003, and Microsoft Windows Server 2008.

The recommended RAM for running Oracle Database XE is 512 MB; however, nowadays most computers are equipped with at least 1 GB of memory. To continue with the database installation make sure you have administrative privilege.

The following Oracle Database XE installation procedure is for the Windows XP operating system. Make the necessary navigational changes if you are using other versions of Microsoft Windows' operating system.

1. Unzip the downloaded Oracle Database XE software into a temporary folder, say `c:\temp`.

2. Navigate to the `Disk1` folder under `c:\temp` and double-click on `setup.exe`. A new window pops up, as shown in the following screenshot:

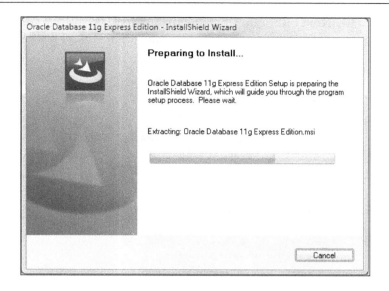

3. Oracle Database XE prepares the install shield wizard and once the preparation completes, the following screen is displayed:

4. Click on the **Next** button to start the installation. Accept the license agreement on the following screen and click on the **Next** button:

5. On the next screen, you may choose an alternative location for your Oracle Database XE installation. However, it is recommended to continue with the default directory. Click on **Next** after choosing the destination directory, as shown in the following screenshot:

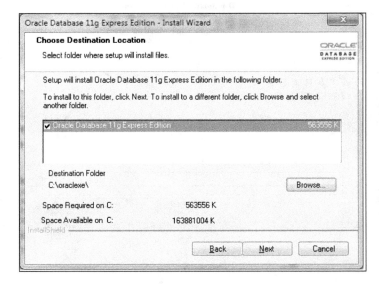

6.  The next screen is shown in the following screenshot; enter the password for SYS and SYSTEM users and click on **Next** to continue:

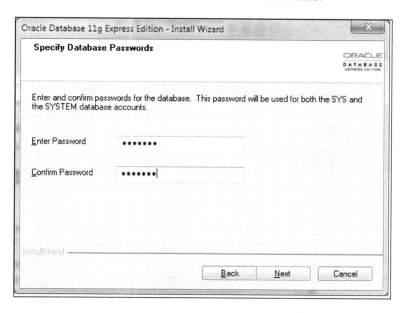

7.  The next screen provides a summary of installation settings, as shown in the following screenshot. Click on the **Install** button to continue installing Oracle Database XE:

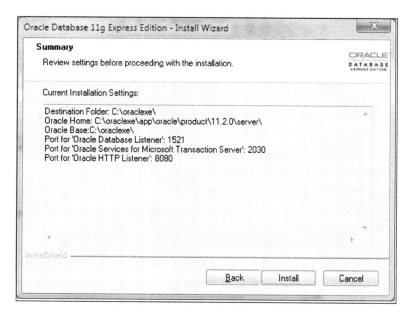

8. The installation begins after you click on the **Install** button and once the installation completes, the following screen appears; this marks the end of installation:

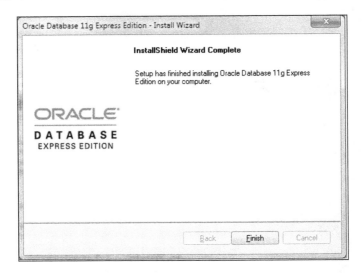

9. Click on **Finish** to complete the installation.

We have successfully installed Oracle Database 11*g* XE. To access the database's home page (shown in the following screenshot) go to **Start | All Programs | Oracle Database 11g Express Edition | Get Started**:

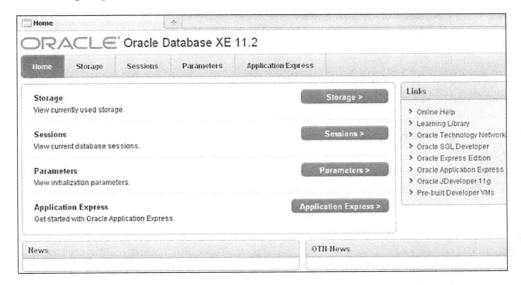

# Starting and stopping Oracle Database XE in Windows

After you have installed Oracle Database XE, the installer creates a Windows service that can be used to start and stop the database.

To stop the running database, go to **Start | All Programs | Oracle Database 11g Express Edition | Stop Database**.

Similarly to start the database, go to **Start | All Programs | Oracle Database 11g Express Edition | Start Database**.

# Uninstalling Oracle Database 11*g* XE on Windows XP (32-bit)

Uninstalling Oracle Database 11*g* XE is the process of removing Oracle Database XE software and the database from the machine. To remove the software and database, navigate to **Start | Control Panel | Add or Remove Programs** . Right-click on **Oracle Database 11g Express Edition** and click on **Remove**.

A confirmation window pops up, as shown in the following screenshot. Click on **Yes** to continue uninstalling:

If Oracle Database 11*g* XE is already running, the uninstallation process first stops the database and then proceeds with removing the database and software.

# Installing Oracle Database 11*g* XE on Oracle Enterprise Linux (64-bit)

Before we begin installing Oracle Database XE in Linux, we need to prepare the environment by installing the required packages, setting kernel parameters, and so on.

To begin, make sure that the following Linux packages are installed. To verify that the following Linux packages are installed use the `rpm -qa <package name>` command:

- `kernel-headers-2.6.18-194.el5.x86_64.rpm`
- `glibc-2.5-49.x86_64.rpm`
- `make-3.81-3.el5.x86_64.rpm`
- `binutils-2.17.50.0.6-14.el5.x86_64.rpm`
- `glibc-devel-2.5-49.x86_64.rpm`
- `glibc-headers-2.5-49.x86_64.rpm`
- `libgomp-4.4.0-6.el5.x86_64.rpm`
- `gcc-4.1.2-48.el5.x86_64.rpm`
- `libaio-0.3.106-5.x86_64.rpm`

The parameters that need to be included in the `sysctl.conf` file under `/etc` are as follows. These changes are to be made by logging in as the `root` user:

```
kernel.semmsl=250
kernel.semmns=32000
kernel.semopm=100
kernel.semmni=128
kernel.shmmax=4294967295
kernel.shmmni=4096
kernel.shmall=2097152
kernel.sem= 250 32000 100 128
fs.file-max= 6815744
net.ipv4.ip_local_port_range=9000 65500
```

We are now ready to start the Oracle Database XE installation. However, it is recommended to complete the following steps for creating a Linux user `oracle`:

1. Create new groups and the `oracle` user as shown in the following code snippet, by logging in as the `root` user:

```
groupadd oinstall
groupadd dba
useradd -g oinstall -G dba,oper,asmadmin oracle
passwd oracle
```

2. Log in as the `oracle` user and add the following lines at the end of the `.bash_profile` file:

```
# Oracle instance name
ORACLE_SID=XE; export ORACLE_SID;
# Oracle home directory
ORACLE_HOME=/u01/app/oracle/product/11.2.0/xe; export ORACLE_HOME;
# Search path for executable
```

```
PATH=$ORACLE_HOME/bin:$PATH; export PATH;
# Search path for shared libraries
LD_LIBRARY_PATH=$ORACLE_HOME/lib:$LD_LIBRARY_PATH; export LD_
LIBRARY_PATH
```

3. Copy the downloaded software to a temporary folder, say /u01/software, and run the following command as the root user to install Oracle Database XE, as shown in the following screenshot:

```
[root@xe1 software]# rpm -ivh oracle-xe-11.2.0-1.0.x86_64.rpm
Preparing...                ########################################### [100%]
   1:oracle-xe              ########################################### [100%]
Executing post-install steps...

You must run '/etc/init.d/oracle-xe configure' as the root user to configure the database.

[root@xe1 software]#
```

4. Run /etc/init.d/oracle-xe configure as the root user to configure the database. You will be prompted to select the HTTP port for Oracle Application Express, database listener port, SYS and SYSTEM user password, and the boot option. It is recommended to accept the default values and continue with the configuration of the database as shown in the following screenshot:

```
[root@xe1 software]# /etc/init.d/oracle-xe configure

Oracle Database 11g Express Edition Configuration
-------------------------------------------------
This will configure on-boot properties of Oracle Database 11g Express
Edition.  The following questions will determine whether the database should
be starting upon system boot, the ports it will use, and the passwords that
will be used for database accounts.  Press <Enter> to accept the defaults.
Ctrl-C will abort.

Specify the HTTP port that will be used for Oracle Application Express [8080]:

Specify a port that will be used for the database listener [1521]:

Specify a password to be used for database accounts.  Note that the same
password will be used for SYS and SYSTEM.  Oracle recommends the use of
different passwords for each database account.  This can be done after
initial configuration:
Confirm the password:

Do you want Oracle Database 11g Express Edition to be started on boot (y/n) [y]:

Starting Oracle Net Listener...Done
Configuring database...Done
Starting Oracle Database 11g Express Edition instance...Done
Installation completed successfully.
[root@xe1 software]#
```

To access the database's home page go to **Applications menu | Oracle Database 11g Express Edition | Get Started**.

# Starting and stopping Oracle Database XE in Linux

After you have installed Oracle Database XE, the database is up and running and you can begin using it right away.

To stop the running database, go to **Applications menu | Oracle Database 11g Express Edition | Stop Database**.

Similarly to start the database, go to **Applications menu | Oracle Database 11g Express Edition | Start Database**.

Alternatively, we can start the database manually by running the following command as the root user:

```
# /etc/init.d/oracle-xe start
```

To manually stop the database, run the following command as the root user:

```
# /etc/init.d/oracle-xe stop
```

# Uninstalling Oracle Database 11*g* XE on Oracle Enterprise Linux (64-bit)

When you uninstall Oracle Database XE, all components, including datafiles, control files, redo logfiles, and software are removed.

Log on with the root privilege and run the command shown in the following screenshot to uninstall Oracle Database XE:

```
[root@xe1 software]#
[root@xe1 software]# rpm -e oracle-xe
[root@xe1 software]#
```

# Summary

After completing this chapter, you should be able to install and uninstall Oracle Database 11*g* XE on both Linux and Windows operating systems. You should be familiar with starting and stopping the database on both the Linux and Windows environments using the respective services/commands. We also had a first look at the Oracle Database 11*g* XE home page.

In the next chapter, we will configure our database for local and remote database connections.

# 3
# Connecting and Configuring Oracle Database 11*g* XE

*Motivation is what gets you started. Habit is what keeps you going. - Unknown*

This chapter focuses on establishing a connection to Oracle Database 11*g* XE from client machines. There are different ways in which you can establish a connection to the database; for example, local and remote connections. We will explore these in detail. Also, we will learn to configure the database listener. Oracle memory management is another topic that will be covered in this chapter. The following topics will be covered in this chapter:

- Local database connections
- Oracle Net Listener
  - ° Configuring Oracle Net Listener
  - ° Viewing the status of Oracle Net Listener
  - ° Starting and stopping the listener
  - ° Configuring the tnsnames.ora file
- Remote database connections
- Changing the SGA and PGA sizes

## Local database connections

Establishing a connection locally means running the SQL command-line utility on the same computer where Oracle Database 11*g* XE is installed, and initiating a database connection command using the valid database credentials.

The following screenshot is taken from Oracle Database 11g XE on Windows, and demonstrates establishing a local database connection to the database:

```
C:\>cd c:\oraclexe\app\oracle\product\11.2.0\server\bin

c:\oraclexe\app\oracle\product\11.2.0\server\bin>
c:\oraclexe\app\oracle\product\11.2.0\server\bin>sqlplus "/nolog"

SQL*Plus: Release 11.2.0.2.0 Production on Wed Dec 21 00:03:58 2011

Copyright (c) 1982, 2010, Oracle.  All rights reserved.

SQL>
SQL> connect system/sys1234
Connected.
SQL>
```

Navigate to the Oracle Database 11g XE database home and start the `sqlplus` session with the `/nolog` option. Using the `connect` statement establish a connection to the database by supplying the valid database username and password. As shown in the preceding screenshot, connect as SYSTEM user with the password entered while installing Oracle Database 11g XE.

ORA_DBA is a local Windows group that gets automatically created when you install Oracle Database XE and your Windows username automatically gets added to this group. Members of ORA_DBA can connect to the Oracle Database XE without a password, as shown in the following screenshot:

```
C:\Users\amomen>sqlplus "/as sysdba"

SQL*Plus: Release 11.2.0.2.0 Production on Tue May 1 13:09:48 2012

Copyright (c) 1982, 2010, Oracle.  All rights reserved.


Connected to:
Oracle Database 11g Express Edition Release 11.2.0.2.0 - Production

SQL>
SQL>
SQL>
SQL> conn /as sysdba
Connected.
SQL>
```

# Oracle Net Listener

To connect to the database remotely, we should have Oracle Net Listener running on the host where Oracle Database 11g XE is installed. When a remote client initiates a database connection request, this connection request is received by Oracle Net Listener. The job of the listener is to listen to these incoming database connection requests and hand over the connection requests to the appropriate databases.

Thereafter the remote-client connection directly communicates with the database without the need of the listener. Without the listener service running we cannot connect to the database remotely. There may be more than one database running on the host server; however, you will only have one database listener for all incoming requests. Based on the incoming request, Oracle Net Listener will hand over the connection request to the appropriate database.

Oracle Net Listener and the tnsnames.ora files are configured by default when we install Oracle Database 11*g* XE. The listener's configuration file is located under $ORACLE_HOME\network\admin\listener.ora. Oracle Database XE automatically creates a Windows service for Oracle Net Listener (OracleXETNSListener).

# Configuring Oracle Net Listener

listener.ora is the name of the Oracle Net Listener configuration file and it resides under $ORACLE_HOME\network\admin.

The content of a sample listener.ora file in its simplest form is as follows:

```
SID_LIST_LISTENER =
  (SID_LIST =
    (SID_DESC =
      (SID_NAME = XE)
      (ORACLE_HOME = C:\oraclexe\app\oracle\product\11.2.0\server)
    )
  )

LISTENER =
  (DESCRIPTION_LIST =
    (DESCRIPTION =
      (ADDRESS = (PROTOCOL = TCP)(HOST = amomen-PC)(PORT = 1521))
    )
  )
```

The description of the parameters is as follows:

- LISTENER: The name of the listener
- SID_NAME: The Oracle Database name
- ORACLE_HOME: The Oracle software installation home directory
- HOST: The name of the host where Oracle Net Listener is running
- PORT: The port on which Oracle Net Listener is listening to the incoming requests

Make the necessary changes to the preceding parameters, save the file, and restart the Windows Oracle Listener service `OracleXETNSListener`.

# Viewing the status of Oracle Net Listener

Navigate to Oracle home (`$ORACLE_HOME\bin`), start the listener utility (`lsnrctl`), enter `status` as shown in the following screenshot, and hit *Enter*.

If the listener is not started, the command displays an error message, as shown in the following screenshot:

```
LSNRCTL>
LSNRCTL> status
Connecting to (DESCRIPTION=(ADDRESS=(PROTOCOL=IPC)(KEY=EXTPROC1)))
TNS-12541: TNS:no listener
 TNS-12560: TNS:protocol adapter error
  TNS-00511: No listener
   32-bit Windows Error: 2: No such file or directory
Connecting to (DESCRIPTION=(ADDRESS=(PROTOCOL=TCP)(HOST=amomen-PC)(PORT=1521)))
TNS-12541: TNS:no listener
 TNS-12560: TNS:protocol adapter error
  TNS-00511: No listener
   32-bit Windows Error: 61: Unknown error
LSNRCTL>
```

If the listener is running, the command displays detailed listener information as shown in the following screenshot:

```
LSNRCTL>
LSNRCTL> status
Connecting to (DESCRIPTION=(ADDRESS=(PROTOCOL=IPC)(KEY=EXTPROC1)))
STATUS of the LISTENER
------------------------
Alias                     LISTENER
Version                   TNSLSNR for 32-bit Windows: Version 11.2.0.2.0 - Production
Start Date                21-DEC-2011 01:41:30
Uptime                    0 days 0 hr. 23 min. 6 sec
Trace Level               off
Security                  ON: Local OS Authentication
SNMP                      OFF
Default Service           XE
Listener Parameter File   C:\oraclexe\app\oracle\product\11.2.0\server\network\admin\listener.ora
Listener Log File         C:\oraclexe\app\oracle\diag\tnslsnr\amomen-PC\listener\alert\log.xml
Listening Endpoints Summary...
  (DESCRIPTION=(ADDRESS=(PROTOCOL=ipc)(PIPENAME=\\.\pipe\EXTPROC1ipc)))
  (DESCRIPTION=(ADDRESS=(PROTOCOL=tcp)(HOST=amomen-PC)(PORT=1521)))
  (DESCRIPTION=(ADDRESS=(PROTOCOL=tcp)(HOST=amomen-PC)(PORT=8080))(Presentation=HTTP)(Session=RAW))
Services Summary...
Service "CLRExtProc" has 1 instance(s).
  Instance "CLRExtProc", status UNKNOWN, has 1 handler(s) for this service...
Service "PLSExtProc" has 1 instance(s).
  Instance "PLSExtProc", status UNKNOWN, has 1 handler(s) for this service...
Service "XEXDB" has 1 instance(s).
  Instance "xe", status READY, has 1 handler(s) for this service...
Service "xe" has 1 instance(s).
  Instance "xe", status READY, has 1 handler(s) for this service...
The command completed successfully
LSNRCTL>
```

# Starting and stopping the listener

The listener is automatically configured when we install Oracle Database 11*g* XE.

- To stop the listener on Windows, launch the **Services** window by navigating to **Start | Control Panel | Administrative Tools | Services** and stop the **OracleXETNSListener** service, or launch the listener utility (lsnrctl) and enter the LSNRCTL> stop command. To stop the listener on Linux, within the listener utility (lsnrctl) enter the stop command as we did in the Windows environment.

- To start the listener on Windows, launch the **Services** window by navigating to **Start | Control Panel | Administrative Tools | Services** and start the **OracleXETNSListener** service, or launch the listener utility (lsnrctl) and enter the LSNRCTL> start command. To start the listener on Linux, within the listener utility (lsnrctl) enter the start command as we did in Windows environment.

# Configuring the tnsnames.ora file

**Transparent Network Susbstrate (TNS)** handles all remote database connections. Oracle software reads the TNS connection string to understand how to connect to the remote databases. Every Oracle database and the Oracle Client software will have this file. By default the tnsnames.ora file is located under $ORACLE_HOME\network\admin. A sample alias entry from the tnsnames.ora file is as follows:

```
MY_XE =
  (DESCRIPTION =
    (ADDRESS = (PROTOCOL = TCP)(HOST = amomen-PC)(PORT = 1521))
    (CONNECT_DATA =
      (SERVER = DEDICATED)
      (SID = XE)
    )
  )
```

In the preceding code:

- MY_XE is an alias name. You can name it anything you like.
- HOST is the hostname or IP-Address where database is running.
- PORT is the port number on which Oracle Net Listener is listening.
- SID is the Oracle database name.

When connecting to the remote database, we will use my_xe as a connect string.

# Remote database connections

Establishing a connection remotely means running the SQL command-line utility on a different host other than the Oracle Database 11*g* XE machine and initiating a database connection command using the valid database credentials over the network using a `connect` string.

The following screenshot is taken from Oracle Database 11*g* XE on Windows, and demonstrates establishing a remote database connection to the database:

```
c:\>
c:\>cd c:\oraclexe\app\oracle\product\11.2.0\server\bin

c:\oraclexe\app\oracle\product\11.2.0\server\bin>
c:\oraclexe\app\oracle\product\11.2.0\server\bin>sqlplus "/nolog"

SQL*Plus: Release 11.2.0.2.0 Production on Wed Dec 21 00:31:15 2011

Copyright (c) 1982, 2010, Oracle.  All rights reserved.

SQL>
SQL> connect system/sys1234@xe
Connected.
SQL>
```

As discussed earlier, a `connect` string defines which database server to connect to, on what port, and using what protocol. In the preceding example, `xe` is the name of the `connect` string.

Alternatively, we can connect to the database by providing the database host name and port as shown in the following screenshot:

```
SQL>
SQL> connect system/sys1234@amomen-pc:1521
Connected.
SQL>
```

The database hostname name and port information is basically encapsulated in the `connect` string.

Using the local `sqlplus` utility we can connect to the database via listener; thus, simulating remote client connections. To achieve this, we need to configure the `tnsnames.ora` file and make sure that the listener is running.

The remote host initiating database connection should have Oracle Client software installed. It is through this client software that the Oracle command-line utilities connect to the database.

You can download Oracle Database 11*g* R2 Client software for Windows from `http://www.oracle.com/technetwork/database/enterprise-edition/downloads/112010-win32soft-098987.html`. To download the software you have to log in and accept the license agreement.

> **Downloading the example code**
>
> You can download the example code files for all Packt books you have purchased from your account at http://www.packtpub.com. If you purchased this book elsewhere, you can visit http://www.packtpub.com/support and register to have the files e-mailed directly to you.

# Changing SGA and PGA sizes

Oracle instance is made up of background processes and the shared memory (SGA). The background processes perform the maintenance tasks that are required to keep the database running. These background processes operate on the allocated shared memory. For example, one of the background process (PMON) is responsible for cleaning up (releasing locks and resources) after abnormally terminated database connections.

There are two types of memory that Oracle instance allocates:

- **System Global Area (SGA)**: This is a shared memory area that contains database buffers, shared SQL and PL/SQL, and other control information for the instance.

- **Process Global Area (PGA)**: This memory is private to a single process. PGA keeps process-specific information such as Oracle shared resources being used by a process, operating system resources used by the process, and other database session related information.

Oracle Database XE uses **Automatic Memory Management (AMM)**. This means Oracle Database XE dynamically manages SGA and PGA memories. AMM uses the `MAX_TARGET` initialization parameters to manage the instance memory. Oracle instance dynamically redistributes the memory between SGA and PGA based on the memory requirements when operating in the AMM mode.

Individual sizes of SGA and PGA can be set using the `SGA_TARGET` and `PGA_AGGREGATE_TARGET` parameters respectively. The maximum amount of memory that Oracle Database 11*g* XE allows for `MEMORY_TARGET` (SGA and PGA together) is 1 GB.

To change AMM memory, and SGA and PGA parameters, set MEMORY_TARGET to 1 GB as shown in the following command:

```
SQL> ALTER SYSTEM SET memory_target = 1G SCOPE=spfile;
System altered.
SQL>
```

1. Set the SGA_TARGET value using the ALTER SYSTEM command as shown in the following screenshot.

2. Set the PGA_AGGREGATE_TARGET value as shown in the following screenshot.

3. Restart the database so that the new values of AMM, SGA, and PGA take effect.

```
SQL>
SQL> alter system set sga_target=600M scope=spfile;

System altered.

SQL>
SQL> alter system set pga_aggregate_target=400M scope=spfile;

System altered.

SQL>
```

# Summary

In this chapter we learned how to establish a database connection on the local host as well as from the remote host. You should now be familiar with the Oracle Net Listener concepts and configuration. In this chapter, we have also learned about Oracle memory management and the procedure to change memory settings.

In the next chapter we will interact with the database by writing SQL queries. Some of the most commonly used SQL functions will also be discussed. We will create a sample table in the next chapter and learn to insert, modify, and delete records from this table.

# 4

# Accessing Table Data, DML Statements, and Transactions

*Always desire to learn something useful. - Sophocles*

In this chapter, we will install Oracle's free graphical tool, SQL Developer and use it to communicate with Oracle Database XE. You use SQL Developer to browse database objects and execute SQL statements. Querying the database is the most common job and this chapter focuses on writing simple and multi-table queries. We will also see some of the common database functions that are used in a daily routine. The following are the topics that are covered in this chapter:

- Unlocking sample user accounts
- Installing SQL Developer
- Connecting SQL Developer to Oracle Database 11*g* XE
- About TAB and DUAL
- Writing simple queries
- Selecting data from multiple tables
- Exploring common functions
- What are Transaction Control Statements?
- Commit Understanding DML statements

## Unlocking sample user accounts

Oracle Database 11*g* XE comes with sample database users such as HR, MDSYS, and others. Some of the user accounts are by default locked. In the rest of the chapters, we will use HR schema objects for our testing and building applications.

Log on to SQL*Plus as SYSDBA, query account status for all users, and unlock the HR account as shown below:

```
SQL> connect /as sysdba
SQL> select username, account_status from dba_users;
SQL> alter user hr account unlock;    # Unlock the locked account
SQL> alter user hr identified by hr;   # Open the expired account
```

Or:

```
SQL> alter user hr identified by hr account unlock; #Unlock and open
in a single statement
SQL> connect hr/hr
```

# Installing SQL Developer

SQL Developer is a graphical tool that enables us to interact with an Oracle database. Using SQL Developer we can query, create/modify/drop database objects, run SQL statements, write PL/SQL stored procedures, and more.

SQL Developer is a separate tool not bundled with Oracle Database 11*g* XE. SQL Developer is free to download. You can download SQL Developer by following this link: http://www.oracle.com/technetwork/developer-tools/sql-developer/.

Installing SQL Developer on Windows and Linux is very straightforward and effortless. The following is the procedure to install in a Windows environment:

1.  Unzip the sqldeveloper-3.1.06.82.zip to a folder.

2.  Navigate to the new folder sqldeveloper created by the ZIP file and double-click on the sqldeveloper.exe file. That's it, we are done.

# Connecting SQL Developer to Oracle Database 11*g* XE

Start SQL Developer and select **Connections** in the pane on the left-hand side and click on the plus symbol to create a new database connection. Now, in the following window that pops up, fill **Connection Name**, **Username**, **Password**, select the checkbox next to **Save Password**, and click on the **Test** button.

Resolve any errors. You should see **Status: Success** above the **Help** button. Save the connection information by clicking on the **Save** button and proceed by clicking on the **Connect** button.

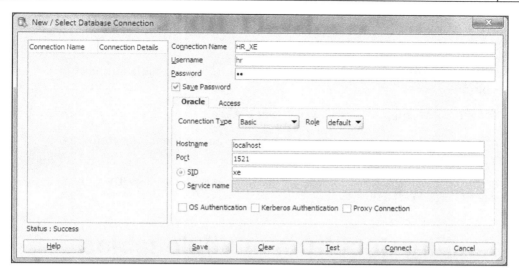

# About TAB and DUAL

DUAL is a SYS owned table. It is normally used to return values from stored functions, sequence values, and so on. It is recommended not to drop or perform any DML operations against a DUAL table. The following is an example of fetching the current date using the DUAL table:

```
SQL> SELECT sysdate FROM dual;

SYSDATE
---------
10-MAY-12

SQL>
```

TAB is a SYS owned view which is used to list tables and views in a table. The following is a sample query to list all tables/views in the current schema:

```
SQL> SELECT * FROM tab;
```

# Writing simple queries

In general, a "query" means a "question". Within the realm of databases, a query fetches information from the database objects such as tables and views. We can combine one or more tables/views in a single query. In this chapter, we will execute queries using the SQL*Plus environment. However, you may prefer to use either SQL Developer or SQL*Plus.

To list columns of a table we use the DESC command in SQL*Plus:

```
SQL> DESC employees
```

Now, let us execute a simple query against the employees table and fetch a few columns:

```
SQL> SELECT employee_id, first_name, last_name, job_id FROM employees;
```

We can restrict the results returned by the query using the WHERE clause as shown below:

```
SQL> SELECT employee_id, first_name, last_name, job_id FROM employees
WHERE salary < 2500;
```

# Selecting data from multiple tables

In the above query, we queried data of the job_id column from the employees table; however, the column values are codes. The actual job description is in the job_title column in the jobs table. The following is a pictorial view of the jobs and employees tables with a pointer to the join columns:

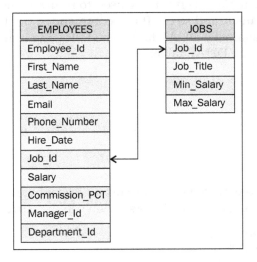

Let us write a query by joining these two tables on the common column job_id to fetch information from both the tables. The query is shown as follows:

```
SELECT e.employee_id, e.first_name, e.last_name, j.job_title
    FROM employees e, jobs j
    WHERE e.job_id = j.job_id;
```

# Exploring common functions

We can use Oracle Supplied functions in our queries. Alternatively, we can create our own functions and later use them in queries. We will learn about functions in the following chapters. In this section, we will explore a few commonly used functions. A complete list of Oracle Supplied functions is out of the scope of this book. You can refer to the Oracle documentation for more details.

Functions in Oracle can be of type scalar or aggregate. Scalar functions operate on a single row whereas the aggregate functions work on multiple rows. In this book we will cover the following Oracle Supplied functions:

| | | | |
|---|---|---|---|
| UPPER | RPAD | MAX | TO_NUMBER |
| LOWER | LPAD | MIN | TO_DATE |
| CONCAT or ("\|\|") | SUBSTR | AVG | |
| LTRIM | COUNT | ADD_MONTHS | |
| RTRIM | SUM | TO_CHAR | |

The UPPER function converts the character string to uppercase. Similarly, the LOWER function converts a given string to lowercase. The following is a sample query from an HR schema:

```
SQL> SELECT UPPER(first_name), LOWER(first_name) FROM employees WHERE
employee_id = 127;

UPPER(FIRST_NAME)    LOWER(FIRST_NAME)
-------------------  -------------------
JAMES                james

SQL>
```

The CONCAT (or "\|\|") function is used to concatenate two character strings into one. The following is an example where the first_name and last_name columns from the employees table are concatenated into one:

```
SQL> SELECT first_name || last_name fullname FROM employees WHERE
employee_id = 127;

FULLNAME
---------------------------------------------
JamesLandry

SQL>
```

The `LTRIM` function removes blank spaces from the left-hand side of the given string:

```
SQL> SELECT '        ' || first_name without_trim,
  2  ltrim( '        ' || first_name) with_trim
  3  FROM employees
  4  WHERE employee_id = 127;


WITHOUT_TRIM                  WITH_TRIM
-------------------------     -------------------------
     James                    James

SQL>
```

We can also use the `LTRIM` function to remove all specified characters from the left-hand side of a string. In the following example, we remove `J` from the `first_name`:

```
SQL> SELECT ltrim( first_name, 'J') FROM employees WHERE employee_id =
127;


LTRIM(FIRST_NAME,'J'
--------------------
ames

SQL>
```

Similarly, the `RTRIM` removes specified characters from the right-hand side of a given string.

The `LPAD` function pads with a specific set of characters to the left-hand side of a string and `RPAD` does the same but on the right-hand side. With these functions, you specify the number of characters and the string to pad. An example query is as follows:

```
SQL> SELECT LPAD(first_name, 10, 'x') lpad_ex, RPAD(first_name, 10,
'x') rpad_ex
  2  FROM employees
  3  WHERE employee_id = 127;


LPAD_EX       RPAD_EX
------------  ------------
xxxxxJames    Jamesxxxxx

SQL>
```

The SUBSTR function is used to extract a portion of the string. We specify how many characters to extract and the starting position. In the following example, we extract 3 characters starting at position 2. So, J and s are not reported in the output. This is done as follows:

```
SQL> SELECT SUBSTR(first_name, 2, 3) FROM employees WHERE employee_id
= 127;

SUBSTR(FIRST
------------
ame

SQL>
```

The COUNT function returns the number of rows in a query and the MAX function returns the maximum value of an expression. Similarly, the MIN and AVG functions return the minimum and average value of the expression respectively. The COUNT, MAX, MIN, and AVG are all aggregated functions as they operate on multiple rows. The following is an example:

```
SQL> SELECT COUNT(*), MIN(salary), MAX(salary), AVG(salary)
  2   FROM employees;

  COUNT(*) MIN(SALARY) MAX(SALARY) AVG(SALARY)
---------- ----------- ----------- -----------
       107        2100       24000  6461.83178

SQL>
```

The ADD_MONTHS function adds the given number of months to the date value and returns a new date, shown as follows:

```
SQL> SELECT hire_date, ADD_MONTHS(hire_date, 2) FROM employees WHERE
employee_id = 127;

HIRE_DATE ADD_MONTH
--------- ---------
14-JAN-07 14-MAR-07

SQL>
```

The `TO_CHAR` function is used to convert a non character value to a character string. `TO_NUMBER` is used to convert a string into a number. However, it raises an error when you try to convert an invalid number. The `TO_DATE` function is used to convert a character string to a date. Again, it raises an error when you try to convert an invalid date. The following is an example:

```
SQL> SELECT  TO_NUMBER('11') tonum,
  2    TO_CHAR('test') tochar,
  3    TO_DATE('01-01-2012', 'dd-mm-yyyy') todate
  4    FROM dual;

    TONUM TOCH TODATE
--------- ---- ---------
       11 test 01-JAN-12

SQL>
```

# What are Transaction Control Statements?

A **transaction** is a sequence of one or more SQL statements treated as one unit. Either all of the statements are performed or none of them are performed. There are two main **Transaction Control Statements (TCS)** , namely `COMMIT` and `ROLLBACK`:

- `COMMIT`: When we `COMMIT` a transaction it means that Oracle has made the change permanent in the database
- `ROLLBACK`: When we `ROLLBACK` a transaction, all the changes performed since the previous `COMMIT`/`ROLLBACK` are all erased

# Understanding DML statements

**Data Manipulation Language** (DML) statements are used to manipulate data in existing tables. `INSERT`, `UPDATE`, and `DELETE` are examples of DML statements. We use `INSERT` to add a new record to the table, `UPDATE` to modify one or more columns of a table, and `DELETE` to remove a record from the table.

The following is an example of an `INSERT` statement. We insert a new record in the `regions` table of the HR schema:

```
SQL> INSERT INTO regions VALUES (5, 'Australia');

1 row created.
```

```
SQL> COMMIT;
Commit complete.
SQL>
```

An example of the UPDATE statement is shown next, where we modify the value of region_name from Australia to Aus and NZ. This is done as follows:

```
SQL> UPDATE regions SET region_name = 'Aus and NZ' Where region_id =
5;

1 row updated.

SQL> COMMIT;
Commit complete.
SQL>
```

The following is an example of the DELETE statement. We remove the newly added record from the regions table as follows:

```
SQL> DELETE FROM regions Where region_id = 5;

1 row deleted.

SQL> COMMIT;
Commit complete.
SQL>
```

Remember that to make the changes permanent we have to commit the transaction.

# Summary

In this chapter we have learned how to interact with Oracle database using SQL*Plus and SQL Developer. This chapter also exposed you to a few commonly used Oracle Supplied functions. We also learned what TCS and DML statements do.

Now that we are familiar with performing DML operations against tables, the next chapter discusses creating and managing tables and indexes. We will also learn about other database objects such as views, sequences, and synonyms.

# References

- Oracle Database SQL Language Reference 11*g* Release 2 (11.2)

# 5
# Creating and Managing Schema Objects

*Only undertake what you can do in an excellent fashion. There are no prizes for average performance. - Brian Tracy*

In this chapter we will discuss various schema objects such as tables, indexes, and views. We will also learn how to create, modify, and drop schema objects using the CREATE, ALTER, and DROP statements. At the end of this chapter, we will discuss the importance of object statistics and how to gather statistics. The topics that will be covered in this chapter are as follows:

- Data Definition Language
- Creating and managing tables
- Creating and managing indexes
- Integrity constraints
- Creating and managing views
- Creating and managing synonyms
- Creating and managing sequences
- Gathering statistics

# Data Definition Language

Statements that create, modify, or change schema objects are termed as **Data Definition Language** (DDL) statements. The CREATE, ALTER, and DROP statements are examples of DDL statements. We create a new schema object using the CREATE statement, modify existing schema objects using the ALTER statement, and remove the schema object from the schema using the DROP statement. We will explore more on DDL statements in the following topics.

The DDL statements can be executed either using SQL*Plus command line or using SQL Developer.

# Creating and managing tables

Tables are the basic unit that store actual user data. Individual data records are referred to as rows, and fields are referred to as columns. Each table consists of one or more columns and rows.

Connect to example HR schema to execute the examples discussed in this chapter. The following is an example of the CREATE statement to create a new table:

```
-- Create a new table
CREATE TABLE emp (
emp_no          NUMBER,         -- Field that will store employee number
emp_name        VARCHAR2(50),    -- Field that will store employee' name
date_of_birth    DATE,         -- This will store employee's date of birth
salary          NUMBER(10,2)    -- Field that will store employee'
salary
);
```

In the preceding code snippet, we have created a new table consisting of four columns. Each column is assigned a data type with respect to the values that it will store. The emp_no column will store only number values, hence the NUMBER data type is assigned. If we have to store an alpha-numeric value, we may consider using VARCHAR2 instead. The VARCHAR2 data type stores variable length alpha-numeric values. The DATE data type stores both date and time.

The NUMBER data type stores positive and negative fixed and floating point numbers. We can optionally specify a precision and scale to the NUMBER data type. The syntax is NUMBER (precision, scale), where "precision" is the total number of digits and "scale" is the number of digits to the right of the decimal point.

As an exercise, you can create other tables to familiarize yourself with the CREATE command.

We will now modify the previously created table to add two new columns. This is achieved by using the ALTER TABLE command. Let us add the nationality and place_of_birth columns to the emp table:

```
-- Modify table to add new columns
ALTER TABLE emp ADD (
nationality     VARCHAR2(30),
place_of_birth     VARCHAR2(30)
);
```

Similarly, we can remove columns from the existing table, as shown in the following code snippet:

```
-- Remove a column from the table
ALTER TABLE emp DROP COLUMN place_of_birth;
```

We will use the DROP TABLE command to remove a table from the schema, as shown in the following code snippet:

```
-- Remove a table
DROP TABLE emp;
```

This command removes the table from the current schema.

Starting with Oracle Database 10*g*, Oracle has implemented a new feature called the recycle bin. All the dropped objects by default move into the recycle bin. This feature is similar to the recycle bin in Microsoft Windows. We can recover dropped tables from recycle bin as we recover deleted files in Microsoft Windows OS, or permanently remove the objects from the recycle bin.

Let us check our recycle bin for any dropped objects:

```
-- Check recyclebin for any dropped objects
SQL> SELECT * FROM recyclebin;
```

You will see our dropped table is now in the recycle bin. To recover the emp table from the recycle bin, we will execute the following command:

```
-- Recover the dropped table
SQL> FLASHBACK TABLE emp TO BEFORE DROP;
Flashback complete.
SQL>
```

The table is recovered from the recycle bin. Querying the `recyclebin` view again returns no records:

```
SQL> select * from recyclebin ;
```

Use the `PURGE` clause with the `DROP TABLE` command to permanently delete a table from the current schema, bypassing the recycle bin:

```
-- Permanently remove a table from the database
SQL> DROP TABLE emp PURGE;
```

# Creating and managing indexes

Indexes are created in a database to quickly locate relevant information. When properly used, indexes will speed SQL execution while reducing disk I/O and memory access. To better understand what an index is, think of the index of words at the back of any book. If you want to quickly locate information, you would refer to the index of words and navigate to that page.

A `rowid` is a pseudo-column that uniquely identifies a row. Each `rowid` contains the following information:

- Object number of the object that the row belongs to
- Data block of the datafile
- Position of the row in the data block
- Datafile number (it resides in)

This information helps an Oracle database to uniquely identify a record.

Indexes in Oracle are schema objects that are stored separately. Each index contains specified values from the indexed column along with the `ROWID` values for the rows that match them.

When accessing a small percentage of the rows of a large table, you would want to use an index. DML statements will become expensive if we have too many indexes, and if we have too few indexes, then queries become expensive. So, the right match has to be established between the two to achieve better performance.

The following is an example to create an index:

```
-- Create a new index
CREATE INDEX salary_idx ON emp(salary);
```

Where `salary_idx` is the name of the index, `emp` is the table name, and `salary` is the column in which the index is created.

Use the ALTER INDEX statement to change or rebuild an existing index. Using the ALTER INDEX statement, we can rename the index, change storage parameters, and change index visibility and usability. You normally rebuild an index when moving it to a different tablespace or when it becomes invalid as the table relocates to a different tablespace. Rebuilding indexes on a regular basis is not required and should not be practiced.

```
-- Rebuild an index
ALTER INDEX salary_idx REBUILD;
```

To drop an index, use the DROP INDEX command, as shown in the following screenshot:

```
-- Permanently remove the index from the database
DROP INDEX salary_idx;
```

# Integrity constraints

Data stored in the database must adhere to certain business rules. An integrity constraint defines a business rule for a table column. When the integrity constraint is enabled, Oracle will enforce the business rule. Integrity constraints are stored as part of table definition within the database.

The following are the integrity constraints:

- NOT NULL: The NOT NULL constraint enforces a column to not accept null values.

- CHECK: The CHECK constraint is used to limit the values that are accepted by a column.

- UNIQUE: The UNIQUE constraint is used to make sure that no duplicate values are entered in the column.

- PRIMARY KEY: The PRIMARY KEY constraint is used to uniquely identify a row in a table. PRIMARY KEY can be thought of as a combination of the UNIQUE key and NOT NULL constraints. Furthermore, a table can have only one primary key.

- FOREIGN KEY: A foreign key column is used to establish link between two tables. The FOREIGN KEY constraint on a column ensures that the value in that column is found in the primary key of another table.

The following is an example of the NOT NULL, CHECK, UNIQUE key, and PRIMARY KEY constraints:

```
-- Create an orders table with different integrity constraints
included
CREATE TABLE orders (
order_no      NUMBER      PRIMARY KEY,
order_date    DATE          NOT NULL,
description    VARCHAR2(30)      UNIQUE,
loc          VARCHAR2(30)      CHECK (loc IN ('LONDON', 'DUBAI',
'DELHI')));
```

Let us create a detailed order table (order_details), which records all the items purchased in a single order. We will then connect the order_details table with the orders table using the FOREIGN KEY constraint:

```
-- Create order details table
CREATE TABLE order_details (
order_no      NUMBER      REFERENCES orders(order_no),
line_no        NUMBER,
item_no      NUMBER,
quantity      NUMBER);
```

In the preceding example, the order_no column of the order_details table refers to the order_no column of the orders table. If we try to insert an order number in order_details, which does not exist in the orders table, the Oracle database will raise an error — **ORA-02291integrity constraint (xx.xxxxx) violated - parent key not found**.

As mentioned earlier in this chapter, there can be only one primary key for a table. However, we can have multiple columns within a primary key. When we define more than one column as our primary key, it is called a **composite primary key**. The following is an example of a composite primary key on the order_details table:

```
-- create composite primary key
ALTER TABLE order_details ADD CONSTRAINT ord_det_pk PRIMARY KEY
(order_no, line_no);
```

# Creating and managing views

A **view** is a stored query. You write a SQL query and save it in the database as a view. A view can reference a single table/view, or multiple tables/views.

The following is an example of the CREATE VIEW statement:

```
-- Create a new view
CREATE [OR REPLACE] VIEW salary_gr_1000 AS
select emp_no, emp_name, salary
FROM emp
WHERE salary > 1000;
```

In the preceding statement, we created a salary_gr_1000 view, which fetches data from the emp table for all employees whose salary is greater than 1000. We can use the OR REPLACE clause to change the query in the view.

We will use the ALTER VIEW statement to compile and modify/drop constraints. The following is an example:

```
-- Compiling view
ALTER VIEW salary_gr_1000 COMPILE;
```

To change the query of a view, we use the CREATE or REPLACE VIEW statement.

Removing a view from the database is achieved using the DROP VIEW statement, as shown in the following code snippet:

```
-- Permanently remove the view from the schema
DROP VIEW salary_gr_1000;
```

# Creating and managing synonyms

A **synonym** is an alternative name for the table or view. A synonym provides data independence and location transparency. The following is an example of the CREATE SYNONYM statement:

```
-- Create a new synonym
CREATE SYNONYM emp_syn FOR emp;
```

Now we can query the emp table directly or using the new emp_syn synonym.

To remove the synonym from the schema, we use the DROP SYNONYM command as follows:

```
-- Permanently remove the synonym from the database
DROP SYNONYM emp_syn;
```

# Creating and managing sequences

A **sequence** is a database object in Oracle that is used to generate a number sequence. Sequences are mostly used for primary key values.

We will create a sequence using the CREATE SEQUENCE statement as follows:

```
-- Create a new sequence
CREATE SEQUENCE emp_seq;
```

After creating a sequence, we can access its values in SQL statements using the CURRVAL and NEXTVAL pseudo-columns. CURRVAL returns the current value of a sequence and NEXTVAL increments the sequence and returns the new value:

```
-- Fetch a new value from emp_seq
SELECT emp_seq.NEXTVAL FROM dual;
-- Query the current value of emp_seq
SELECT emp_seq.CURRVAL FROM dual;
```

Sequences in their simplest form increment by one; however, we can create a sequence to increment/decrement by any value.

We can modify a sequence using the ALTER SEQUENCE statement to change the increment and other sequence properties. This statement affects only future sequence numbers. The following is an example of the ALTER SEQUENCE statement to change the sequence increment from default 1 to 2:

```
-- Modify sequence to increment by "2"
ALTER SEQUENCE emp_seq INCREMENT BY 2;
```

The new values fetched from emp_seq will get incremented by 2.

To drop a sequence from the schema, we use the DROP SEQUENCE statement as follows:

```
-- Permanently remove the sequence from the database
DROP SEQUENCE emp_seq;
```

# Gathering statistics

Statistics are the primary source of information for Oracle Optimizer. It is through the use of statistics that the optimizer attempts to determine the most efficient way to use resources to satisfy our query. The more accurate our statistics are, the better the optimizer's plan choice will be, and thus, the better our query performance will be.

To gather object statistics, we would use the DBMS_STATS package. The following is an example of gathering table statistics:

```
-- Collect table statistics and all indexes that are created on that
table
SQL> EXEC  DBMS_STATS.GATHER_TABLE_STATS('hr', 'emp', estimate_percent
=> 100, cascade => TRUE);
```

The `estimate_percent` parameter tells Oracle to estimate statistics based on a sample. In this example, we are directing Oracle to use 100 percent of the table data to collect statistics. `cascade` tells Oracle to collect table statistics as well as statistics on the dependent objects, for example, indexes. `TRUE` means to collect fresh statistics for all indexes of this table.

The following is an example to gather index statistics:

```
-- Collect statistics on an index
SQL> EXEC  DBMS_STATS.GATHER_INDEX_STATS('hr', 'emp_pk');
```

The following is an example to gather statistics for all the schema objects:

```
SQL> EXEC  DBMS_STATS.GATHER_SCHEMA_STATS('hr');
```

Similarly, to gather statistics for all the objects in the database, you would use the following line of code:

```
SQL> EXEC  DBMS_STATS.GATHER_DATABASE_STATS;
```

There are many ways to gather statistics, some of which are out of the scope of this book. Refer to *Managing Statistics for Optimal Query Performance* by Karen Morton.

# Summary

In this chapter we have learned about DDL statements: creating, modifying, and dropping database objects such as tables, indexes, views, synonyms, and sequences. We also learned the importance of statistics gathering and saw a few techniques to collect statistics.

The next chapter is all about PL/SQL coding. It will introduce you to the basics of PL/SQL programming. You will learn about the stored procedure, functions, and packages. You will also be able to write triggers on the tables by the end of the chapter. Exception handling is one of the most important components of PL/SQL programming and will be covered in the next chapter.

# References

- *Managing Statistics for Optimal Query Performance* by Karen Morton (http://method-r.com/downloads/cat_view/38-papers)

# 6

# Developing Stored Subprograms and Triggers

*The way you give your name to others is a measure of how much you like and respect yourself. -Brian Tracy*

This chapter brings you the power of PL/SQL within your database. Stored subprograms offer distinct advantages over embedding queries in your applications as stored subprograms are more modular and tuneable. We will learn about stored procedures, functions, and packages in this chapter. Error handling is a very critical part of a program and hence is of greater importance. The following topics are discussed in this chapter:

- PL/SQL data types
- Stored subprograms
- Creating stored subprograms
- About packages
- Creating packages
- Wrapping the PL/SQL code
- Exception handling
- PL/SQL triggers

# PL/SQL data types

PL/SQL provides many predefined data types. The most commonly used PL/SQL data types include NUMBER, INTEGER, VARCHAR2, DATE, and BOOLEAN. You assign values to variables using ":=". An example PL/SQL block, that declares variables and assigns some values, is as follows:

```
DECLARE
  l_hire_date    DATE;
  l_ssn          NUMBER;
  l_marital_flag BOOLEAN;       -- True -> Married, False -> Unmarried
  l_name   VARCHAR2(30);
BEGIN
  l_hire_date := TO_DATE('02-03-2001', 'dd-mm-yyyy');
  l_ssn   := 12345678;
  l_marital_flag := TRUE;
  l_name := 'Tom';
END;
/
```

# Stored subprograms

Subprograms are named PL/SQL blocks that can take parameters and be invoked. Subprograms are either functions or procedures and can be compiled and stored in an Oracle database, ready to be executed. Once compiled it is a schema object known as a stored procedure or stored function. Generally, you use a function to compute a value and a procedure to perform a business action.

# Creating stored subprograms

You create a stored subprogram using the CREATE PROCEDURE command. In this section, let us create a sample stored procedure in the HR schema and name it salary_increment. The stored procedure does the following:

1. Accepts EMP_NO as input.
2. Fetches the current salary of the employee.
3. Calculates the increment on the salary.
4. If the salary is greater than 1000 then raise it by 2 percent. If the salary is between 501 and 999, increment it by 5 percent, and if the salary is less than or equal to 500, increment it by 10 percent.
5. Increment the salary of the given employee in the EMP table.
6. Commits the changes.

The following is a screenshot of a PL/SQL stored procedure:

```
SQL> CREATE OR REPLACE PROCEDURE salary_increment (p_emp_no IN emp.emp_no%TYPE) IS
  2    l_salary emp.salary%TYPE;
  3  BEGIN
  4    -- Fetch current salary
  5    SELECT salary INTO l_salary
  6      FROM emp
  7     WHERE emp_no = p_emp_no;
  8
  9    -- If salary is greater than 1000 then give 2 percent increment
 10    IF l_salary > 1000 THEN
 11      l_salary := l_salary + (l_salary * 2 / 100);
 12
 13    -- If salary is greater than 500 then give 5 percent increment
 14    ELSIF l_salary > 500 THEN
 15      l_salary := l_salary + (l_salary * 5 / 100);
 16
 17    -- Otherwise give 10 percent increment
 18    ELSE
 19      l_salary := l_salary + (l_salary * 10 / 100);
 20    END IF;
 21
 22    -- Update the salary
 23    UPDATE emp SET salary = l_salary
 24      WHERE emp_no = p_emp_no;
 25
 26    COMMIT;
 27
 28  END;
 29  /

Procedure created.

SQL>
```

At this point you should be able to successfully create the `salary_increment` procedure. Before we execute this procedure, let us make a note of the salary of "Tom Green" by querying the EMP table. The following screenshot shows the query:

```
SQL> SELECT * FROM emp WHERE emp_no = 4;

    EMP_NO EMP_NAME                         DATE_OF_B      SALARY    DEPT_NO
---------- ----------------------------- ----------- ---------- ----------
         4 Tom Green                        01-FEB-82          80

SQL>
```

From the query shown in the preceding screenshot, we know that the salary of **Tom Green** is **80**. After executing the `salary_increment` procedure, the salary should get incremented to "88". We will execute the procedure in SQL*Plus using the EXECUTE command (in short EXEC), as shown in the following screenshot:

```
SQL> EXEC salary_increment(4);

PL/SQL procedure successfully completed.

SQL>
```

The `salary_increment` procedure has successfully completed, meaning the salary of **Tom Green** should now reflect the incremented salary. Use the SELECT statement to confirm the change, as shown in the following screenshot:

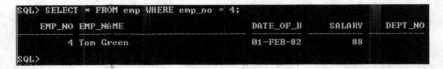

```
SQL> SELECT * FROM emp WHERE emp_no = 4;
    EMP_NO EMP_NAME                        DATE_OF_B    SALARY    DEPT_NO
         4 Tom Green                       01-FEB-82        88
SQL>
```

Note that while creating the procedure I have used CREATE OR REPLACE instead of CREATE. By specifying OR REPLACE while creating the procedure, you ask Oracle to overwrite any already existing procedures. You can use this clause to change the definition of the existing procedure without dropping, recreating, and re-granting object privileges.

Now, let's create a stored function. As mentioned earlier, a stored function is normally used to compute a value. A stored function must include a RETURN statement to return the computed value. The following screenshot shows a sample stored function which returns the name of the given department:

```
SQL> CREATE OR REPLACE FUNCTION get_dept_name(p_department_id IN departments.department_id%TYPE)
  2      RETURN VARCHAR2 IS
  3      l_department_name departments.department_name%TYPE;
  4  BEGIN
  5      SELECT department_name INTO l_department_name
  6          FROM departments
  7          WHERE department_id = p_department_id;
  8
  9      RETURN(l_department_name);
 10  END get_dept_name;
 11  /

Function created.

SQL>
```

Unlike stored procedures, you execute a function within a SQL statement or in an expression. A screenshot of executing the stored function within the SQL statement is as follows:

```
SQL> select get_dept_name(10) from dual;

GET_DEPT_NAME(10)
-----------------
Administration

SQL>
```

To list stored subprograms in your schema query the USER_PROCEDURES view, shown as follows:

```
-- Query to list all objects in a schema ordered by object_type
SQL> SELECT object_name, object_type FROM user_procedures;
```

You can also fetch this information by querying the USER_OBJECTS view.

Query USER_SOURCE to retrieve the source code from the database, shown as follows:

```
-- Query body of stored procedure/function/package/package body
SQL> SELECT text FROM user_source WHERE name = 'GET_DEPT_NAME' ORDER BY
line;
```

Dropping a procedure is a process which will permanently remove a procedure from an Oracle database. The commands to drop stored procedures and functions are as follows:

```
-- Drop stored procedure "salary_increment"
SQL> DROP PROCEDURE salary_increment;
-- Drop stored function "get_dept_name"
SQL> DROP FUNCTION get_dept_name;
```

# About packages

A **package** is a group of logically related procedures, functions, variables, and SQL statements created as a single unit. A package is a schema object just like a table and a sequence. A package has two parts, **package specification** and **package body**.

A package specification does not contain any code. You typically declare variables, constants, cursors, procedures, and functions in a package. A package body is used to provide the implementation details. All the program logic is coded in the body. Within the package specification, we can specify which subprograms are visible to the public and which are not (private). By hiding implementation details from users, you can protect the integrity of the package.

Stored subprograms defined within a package are known as packaged subprograms.

# Creating packages

You create a package specification using the CREATE PACKAGE or CREATE OR REPLACE PACKAGE command. As mentioned earlier, a package is a group of related procedures and functions, so let us create a database package by combining the previously created stored procedure (salary_update) and the stored function (get_dept_name), shown as follows:

```
-- Create package specification
SQL> CREATE OR REPLACE PACKAGE emp_pack IS
  2     -- Function to retrieve department name
```

```
   3    FUNCTION get_dept_name(p_department_id IN departments.department_
id%TYPE) RETURN VARCHAR2;

   4    -- Increment salary

   5    PROCEDURE salary_increment (p_emp_no IN emp.emp_no%TYPE);

   6

7  ENDemp_pack;

8  /
```

You can code and compile a package specification without its body.

Use the CREATE PACKAGE BODY or CREATE OR REPLACE PACKAGE BODY statement to create the package body. The following SQL statement creates the body of the emp_pack package:

```
-- Create package body

SQL> CREATE OR REPLACE PACKAGE BODY emp_pack IS

   2

   3    FUNCTION get_dept_name(p_department_id IN departments.department_
id%TYPE)

   4        RETURN VARCHAR2 IS

   5        l_department_namedepartments.department_name%TYPE;

   6    BEGIN

   :

   :

12    END get_dept_name;

13

14    PROCEDURE salary_increment (p_emp_no IN emp.emp_no%TYPE) IS

15        l_salaryemp.salary%TYPE;

16    BEGIN

   :

   :

41    ENDsalary_increment;

42

43  ENDemp_pack;

44  /
```

Dropping the package and its body is achieved using the DROP PACKAGE and DROP PACKAGE BODY statements respectively. These SQL statements will remove the package/package body permanently from the user schema.

# Exception handling

An exception is an error which arises during the program execution. When an exception is raised, the normal program execution stops and the control transfers to the exception handling section if it exists; otherwise the program stops abruptly. There are two types of exceptions found in Oracle: predefined exceptions and user defined exception.

The predefined exceptions are raised automatically whenever there is a violation of Oracle coding rules, such as NO_DATA_FOUND being raised if a SELECT INTO statement returns no rows. For a complete list of predefined exceptions refer to Oracle Database PL/SQL Language Reference 11*g* Release 2.

Apart from the predefined exceptions, we can explicitly define exceptions based on business rules. These are known as user-defined exceptions. For example, an employee should be at least 18 years old; if he/she is less than 18 then the application should raise an error.

The stored procedure and function created in the previous sections do not include an exception handling section. If you happen to execute the procedure for a non-existent employee then the program fails abruptly with the **ORA-01403 no data found** error.

Let us re-create the stored procedure by including an exception block as shown in the following screenshot:

```
SQL> CREATE OR REPLACE PROCEDURE salary_increment (p_emp_no IN emp.emp_no%TYPE) IS
  2    l_salary emp.salary%TYPE;
  3  BEGIN
  4    -- Fetch current salary
  5    SELECT salary INTO l_salary
  6      FROM emp
  7     WHERE emp_no = p_emp_no;
  8
  9    -- If salary is greater than 1000 then give 2 percent increment
 10    IF l_salary > 1000 THEN
 11      l_salary := l_salary + (l_salary * 2 / 100);
 12
 13    -- If salary is greater than 500 then give 5 percent increment
 14    ELSIF l_salary > 500 THEN
 15      l_salary := l_salary + (l_salary * 5 / 100);
 16
 17    -- Otherwise give 10 percent increment
 18    ELSE
 19      l_salary := l_salary + (l_salary * 10 / 100);
 20    END IF;
 21
 22    -- Update the salary
 23    UPDATE emp SET salary = l_salary
 24      WHERE emp_no = p_emp_no;
 25
 26    COMMIT;
 27
 28  EXCEPTION
 29    WHEN NO_DATA_FOUND THEN
 30      DBMS_OUTPUT.PUT_LINE('Employee does not exist !!!');
 31  END;
 32  /

Procedure created.

SQL>
```

Now when you try to execute the stored procedure with a non-existent employee number, you get a message **Employee does not exist !!!** as shown in the following screenshot:

```
SQL> SET SERVEROUTPUT ON
SQL>
SQL> exec salary_increment(400);
Employee does not exist !!!

PL/SQL procedure successfully completed.

SQL>
```

# Wrapping up the PL/SQL stored programs

You do not always want your code to be displayed in clear text to the outside world. The code may contain proprietary information which needs to be guarded from external sources. Or you may simply want your code to be hidden from the end users to avoid any unofficial code modifications. Oracle provides a PL/SQL wrapper utility for hiding your code. The following steps are required to wrap your code:

1. Save your code (procedure, function, or package) in a text file.
2. Wrap the code using the PL/SQL wrapper utility. A wrapped PL/SQL code file is created by the utility.

Save the `salary_increment` procedure in a text file (say, `c:\salary_increment`) and invoke the PL/SQL wrapper utility in the operating system as shown in the following screenshot:

```
C:\Users\amomen>wrap iname=C:\Temp\salary_increment.sql oname=C:\Temp\salary_increment_wrapped.sql
PL/SQL Wrapper: Release 11.2.0.2.0- Production on Sat Apr 21 16:10:26 2012
Copyright (c) 1993, 2009, Oracle.  All rights reserved.
Processing C:\Temp\salary_increment.sql to C:\Temp\salary_increment_wrapped.sql
C:\Users\amomen>
```

You can run the output file (`c:\temp\salary_increment_wrapped.sql`) as a script in SQL*Plus. For example:

```
-- Execute the wrapped SQL code
SQL> @c:\temp\salary_increment_wrapped.sql
```

# PL/SQL triggers

Triggers are SQL and PL/SQL blocks which are implicitly executed by Oracle when a INSERT, UPDATE, or DELETE statement is issued against the associated table. You cannot explicitly invoke a trigger; however, you can enable and disable a trigger.

A trigger has three basic parts:

- **Triggering event or statement**: This can be a INSERT, UPDATE, or DELETE statement on a table
- **Timing point**: Determines whether the trigger fires before or after the triggering statement and whether it fires for each row that the triggering statement affects
- **Trigger action**: This is the procedure that contains the SQL & PL/SQL statements and code to be run

There are two ways of firing a trigger. Firstly, fire the trigger once for the triggering statement irrespective of how many rows it affects and secondly, once for every row affected. A row trigger is fired for each row while a statement trigger is fired once on behalf of the triggering statement. For example, if the UPDATE statement modifies five rows of a given table, the row trigger fires once for each row (five times) and the statement trigger fires only once.

PL/SQL triggers have four basic timing points:

- **Before the statement**: A trigger can be defined using the BEFORE keyword. Fires only once before the statement.
- **Before each row**: A trigger can be defined using both the BEFORE keyword and the FOR EACH ROW clause. Fires once for each row before it is affected.
- **After each row**: A trigger can be defined using both the AFTER keyword and the FOR EACH ROW clause. Fires once for each row after it is affected.
- **After the statement**: After executing the triggering statement and applying any deferred integrity constraints, the trigger action is executed.

We can combine multiple triggering events (INSERT, UPDATE, and DELETE) in a single trigger and using the conditional predicates we can identify which event has fired the trigger. The conditional predicates are as follows:

- INSERTING: Indicates a INSERT statement fired the trigger
- UPDATING: Indicates a UPDATE statement fired the trigger
- DELETING: Indicates a DELETE statement fired the trigger

A trigger that fires at row level can access the data in the row that it is processing by using correlation names. The default correlation names are OLD and NEW, also called **psuedorecords**.

The OLD and NEW fields for the row that the triggering statement is processing, are as follows:

- INSERT: The OLD value is NULL and NEW contains the post-insert value
- UPDATE: The OLD value contains the pre-update value and NEW contains the post-update value
- DELETE: The OLD value contains the pre-delete value and NEW is NULL

Triggers are commonly used to:

- Log events
- Maintain synchronous table replicas
- Provide auditing
- Prevent invalid transactions
- Enforce complex business rules

Let us create a trigger on the EMP table to log all DML activities performed against it. To achieve this we have to first create a log table, EMP_LOG, as shown in the following screenshot:

```
-- Create a log table
SQL>CREATE TABLE emp_log( emp_no NUMBER, Action VARCHAR2(10), date_
created DATE);
```

This table will record all the actions performed against each and every employee record, along with the date.

Now is the time to create the trigger. You create a trigger using the CREATE TRIGGER statement. The following screenshot shows the SQL statement to create the trigger:

```
SQL> CREATE OR REPLACE TRIGGER emp_log_after_row
  2  AFTER INSERT OR UPDATE OR DELETE ON emp
  3  FOR EACH ROW
  4  BEGIN
  5     -- Insert a record in the log table after every INSERT statement
  6  IF INSERTING THEN
  7     INSERT INTO emp_log VALUES (:NEW.emp_no, 'Insert', SYSDATE);
  8
  9     -- Insert a record in the log table after every DELETE statement
 10  ELSIF DELETING THEN
 11     INSERT INTO emp_log VALUES (:OLD.emp_no, 'Delete', SYSDATE);
 12
 13     -- Insert a record in the log table after every UPDATE statement
 14  ELSIF UPDATING THEN
 15     INSERT INTO emp_log VALUES (:NEW.emp_no, 'Update', SYSDATE);
 16  END IF;
 17
 18  END;
 19  /

Trigger created.

SQL>
```

The trigger is now ready. Let us test the trigger by inserting a new employee (INSERT), modifying the salary of the newly added employee (UPDATE), and then removing the newly added record (DELETE). The SQL statements for these triggers are as follows:

```
-- Add a new employee to the EMP table
SQL>INSERT INTO emp VALUES (99, 'test', SYSDATE, 100, 10);
SQL>COMMIT;


-- Modify the salary of newly added employee
SQL>UPDATE emp SET salary = 800 WHERE emp_no = 99;
SQL>COMMIT;


-- Remove the newly added employee from the EMP table
SQL>DELETE FROM emp WHERE emp_no = 99;
SQL>COMMIT;
```

As mentioned earlier, triggers are fired automatically by Oracle when the triggering event occurs. Our EMP_LOG table should now contain three records—one for the INSERT statement, one for the UPDATE statement, and one for the DELETE statement. The following screenshot illustrates this scenario:

```
SQL> select * from emp_log;

    EMP_NO ACTION    DATE_CREA
---------- --------- ---------
        99 Insert    22-APR-12
        99 Update    22-APR-12
        99 Delete    22-APR-12
SQL>
```

The source code of the database triggers can be retrieved from the USER_TRIGGERS view or from the USER_SOURCE view.

Like stored procedures, we use the CREATE OR REPLACE statement to modify trigger definition. However, we can enable and disable the triggers using the following statement:

```
-- Disable the trigger
SQL> ALTER TRIGGER emp_log_after_row DISABLE;
```

```
-- Enable the trigger
SQL> ALTER TRIGGER emp_log_after_row ENABLE;
```

By default, the CREATE TRIGGER creates the trigger in an enabled state. A trigger will not fire when it is in a disabled state. You may want to disable a trigger when performing a large data load.

Dropping the trigger will remove it permanently from the database and is achieved using the DROP TRIGGER statement, shown as follows:

```
-- Dropping the trigger
SQL> DROP TRIGGER emp_log_after_row;
```

You can also create triggers at schema and database level. These triggers are called **system triggers**. A database trigger can be used to alter session parameters, to audit user logons, and other such tasks. An example usage of a schema trigger is to code a triggering event preventing users from dropping any objects within the schema. More information system triggers can be accessed from Oracle documentation.

# Summary

In this chapter, we have learned about stored procedures, functions, and packages. We know how to create, modify, and drop the stored procedures. Also, in this chapter you were exposed to error handling techniques. Wrapping your code is another great feature of the Oracle database to protect your hard work from getting copied by unauthorized users. We have also seen database triggers in action.

The next chapter will introduce you to Oracle's free development tool—Oracle Application Express (APEX). In this chapter, we will understand APEX components. We will use APEX to browse and manage schema objects. We will also develop a small application using APEX.

# References

- Oracle Database PL/SQL Language Reference 11g Release 2

# 7

# Building a Sample Application with Oracle Application Express

*It is better for a leader to make a mistake in forgiving than to make a mistake in punishing. - Prophet Muhammad*

This chapter provides a brief introduction to Oracle **Application Express** (**APEX**) and its components. We will also learn how to create a workspace followed by a sample application. Step-by-step instructions will show how to load/unload data to/from the database using APEX. At the end of the chapter you should be able to develop small applications using APEX and get familiar with all the APEX components. The topics that will be covered in this chapter are as follows:

- What is Oracle Application Express (APEX)?
- Getting started with Oracle Application Express
- Application Express components
- Prerequisites of a sample application
- Creating a sample application
- Adding a page to an existing application
- Creating application users
- Loading and unloading data to a text file
- Application Express Dashboard

# What is Oracle Application Express (APEX)?

APEX is a browser-based **Rapid Application Development (RAD)** tool that helps you to create rich, interactive Oracle-based web applications. APEX is installed with Oracle Database 11*g* XE by default. APEX is a no-cost option for the Oracle database. Instead of downloading APEX you can sign up for an account on Oracle's hosted version of APEX at `http://apex.oracle.com`.

# Getting started with Oracle Application Express

To start using APEX, we must create a workspace. Each workspace represents a private container in which developers create and deploy their APEX applications. A **workplace** is a group of applications, each containing one or more pages.

The first step in building an application using APEX is to create a workspace. To create a workspace in a freshly installed Oracle Database 11*g* XE, follow these steps:

1.  Launch the **Get Started** page.

2.  Click on **Application Express**.

3.  Create a new application express user **apex_hr** for the existing **HR** database user as shown in the following screenshot:

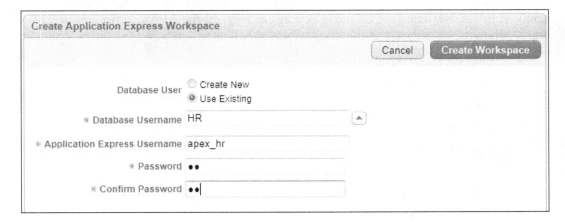

4.  Click on **Create Workspace**.

5.  On the next page that appears, click on the **Click Here** button to log in to the workspace.

# Application Express components

The application express consists of the following four components:

- **Application Builder**: Using this component, you can build database and websheet applications. Application Developers build applications using database applications. Using websheet applications, end users can manage structured and unstructured data without developer assistance.

- **SQL Workshop**: This component provides the following tools that enable you to view and manage database objects:
    - ° **Object Browser**: This tool allows you to browse database objects. You can also create database objects such as tables, sequences, and triggers.
    - ° **SQL Commands**: You can run ad-hoc SQL commands using this tool. The SQL Scripts tool enables you to store and run SQL scripts.
    - ° **Query Builder**: Using this tool, you can create SQL queries using drag-and-drop.
    - ° **Utilities**: This tool enables you to load and unload data, generate DDLs for the database objects, and supports schema comparison.

- **Team Development**: This component helps to manage the lifecycle of an application's development. It is tightly integrated with the APEX Application Builder.

- **Administration**: This component provides service management, user management, and workspace activity.

# Prerequisites for a sample application

In this section, we will discuss the prerequisites for creating the sample application. We will base our application on the HR.EMP table created in *Chapter 5, Creating and Managing Schema Objects*. Add a primary key constraint to the EMP table. We will create a database sequence; this will be used to autogenerate unique numbers for the EMP_NO column. We will then create a database trigger on the EMP table, which will assign the unique number generated by the sequence to the EMP_NO column. The process to be followed is:

1. Create a table emp using the CREATE TABLE command:

```
-- Create a new table
CREATE TABLE emp (
emp_no NUMBER,  -- Field that will store employee number
emp_name VARCHAR2(50),  -- Field that will store employee's name
```

```
date_of_birth DATE,   -- Field that will store employee's date of
birth
salary NUMBER(10,2)   -- Field that will store employee' salary
);
```

2.  Now, create a primary key constraint:

```
-- Create a Primary Key Constraint
ALTER TABLE emp ADD CONSTRAINT emp_pk PRIMARY KEY (emp_no);
```

3.  The next step is to create a database sequence; we will use the autogenerated unique numbers for EMP_NO:

```
CREATE SEQUENCE emp_seq;
```

You can also create the above sequence using Object Builder. Navigate to Object Builder (**Application Express Home | SQL Workshop | Object Browser**). Click on the **Create** button and select **Sequence**. The following screen appears; enter the sequence name leaving other columns at their default values:

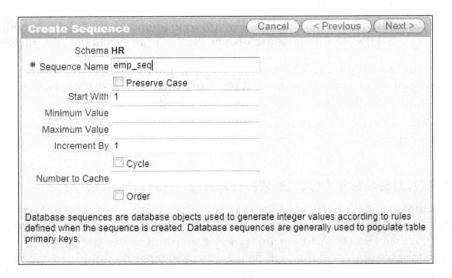

4.  Click on **Next** to continue. The following screen appears with the SQL statement. Click on the **Create** button and we are done creating the sequence (**EMP_SEQ**).

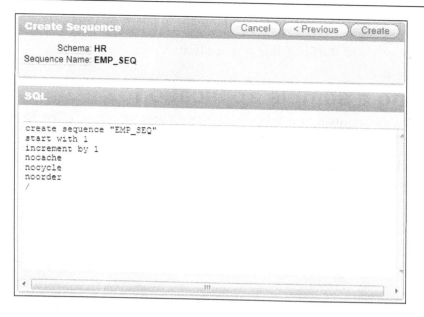

5. The last step is to create a database trigger on the **EMP** table. Select **Tables** from the dropdown list on the left-hand pane. Click on the **EMP** table and then click on the **Triggers** link. Now click on the **Create** button. A new screen appears. Select **insert** for the **Options** column from the dropdown list. In the **Trigger Body** section assign the next sequence number to the emp_no column, as shown in the following screenshot:

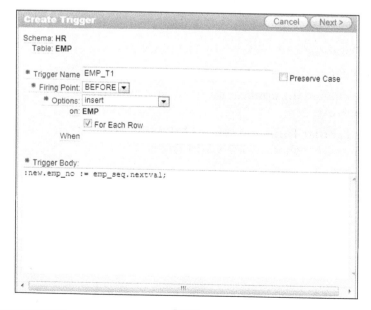

6. Click on the **Next** button to complete the creation process.

Now we are ready to start building our application.

# Creating a sample application

Now that the prerequisites are taken care of, we are ready to start developing our first application:

1. Click on **Application Builder** and select **Create**. The following screenshot shows what you will see:

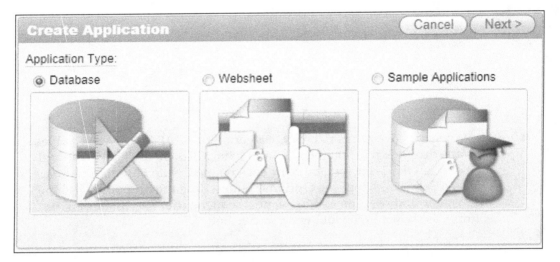

2. Select **Database** and click on the **Next** button.
3. On the next screen, select **From Scratch** and click on **Next**.
4. You can change the application name and application ID (this is optional). Click on **Next**.
5. Choose **Tabular Form** and select **EMP** for the table name as shown in the following screenshot; click on **Add Page**:

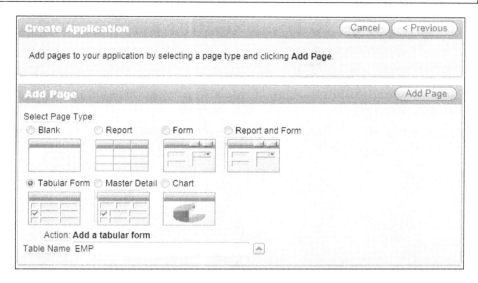

6. A new page gets added to the application. Click on the **Create** button.

7. The next screen displays the selections made. Click on the **Create** button to create the application.

We have now completed creating the application and it is time to run the application. Click on the **Run Application** button and log in to the application using your Apex credentials. Click on the **Add Row** button to add a new record to the **EMP** table and click on the **Submit** button. I have added two records to the **EMP** table as shown in the following screenshot:

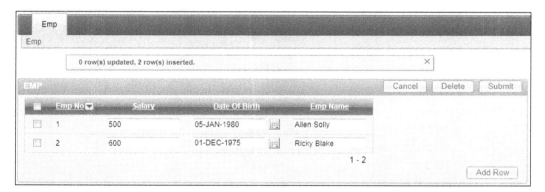

You can add a few more records using the same screen. Also try to modify and delete a few records.

# Adding a page to the existing application

Let us take our application a step further by adding a new page. To create a new page, follow these steps:

1. Click on **Application Builder**. Now click on the application we created in the previous section.

2. Click on the **Create Page** button displayed at the top-right side as shown in the following screenshot:

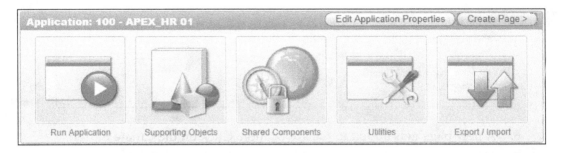

3. On the next screen that appears select **Chart** and click on **Next**. Select **HTML Chart** on the next screen and click on **Next**.

4. Accept the default values on the **Chart details** screen and click on **Next**.

5. You will see the following screen. Select the **Use an existing tab set and create a new tab within the existing tab set** option and name the tab **Salary Chart**. Click on **Next**.

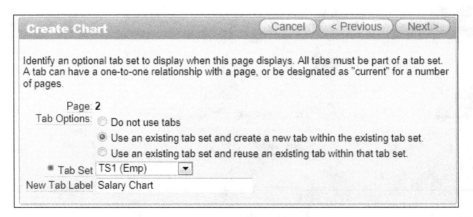

6. On the next screen, change the default SQL query as shown in the following screenshot and click on **Next**:

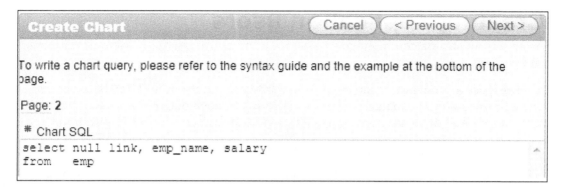

7. Click on the **Finish** button to add the new page to the application. You will receive a message confirming successful creation of the new page. Click on the **Run Page** button.

8. When the application runs, you will notice two tabs — **Emp** and **Salary Chart**. Navigate between the two tabs by clicking on the tab name. This chart is shown in the following screenshot:

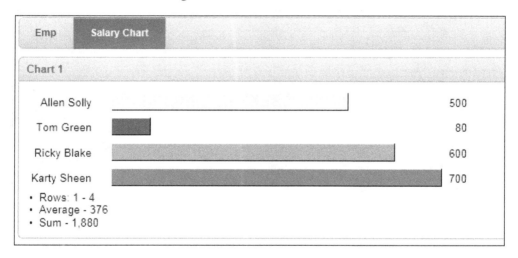

There are many options to explore while creating an application which are out of the scope of this book. Refer to the Oracle Application Express documentation for more details.

# Creating application users

As an administrator you manage workspace administrators, application developers, and end users.

A workspace administrator can create and modify applications and database objects. The administrator also manages users and groups. A developer can create and modify applications and database objects, while the end user can only access applications.

An example of creating an application user is as follows:

1. Navigate to **Application Express Home | Administration | Manage Users and Groups**.
2. Click on the **Create User** button.
3. Enter the **User identification** details.
4. Select **No** for the **User is a workspace administrator** option and **Yes** for **User is a developer**, as shown in the following screenshot. Click on the **Create User** button:

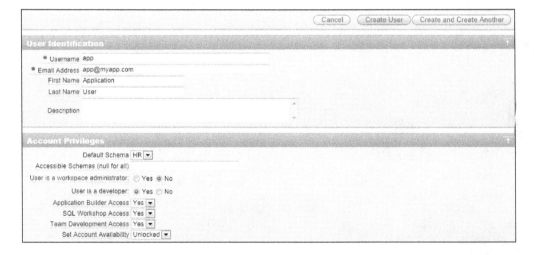

Similarly, you can create workspace administrators and end users.

# Loading and unloading data to a text file

This section describes how to use Oracle Application Express utilities to load and unload data from Oracle Database. **Unloading** is a process of copying table data to external files while **loading** is a process of copying data from external files to a database table.

# Unloading the EMP table to a text file

You can use the **Unload** page to export table data as a text file. To unload the **EMP** table to a text file, follow this process:

1. Navigate to the **Unload** page (**Workspace home page** | **SQL Workshop** | **Utilities** | **Data workshop** | **Data Unload** | **To Text**)

2. Select the **HR** schema and click on the **Next** button.

3. Select the **EMP** table from the dropdown list and click on the **Next** button.

4. Select all the columns.

5. Choose the default values for **Separator**, select **Include Column Names and other columns,** and click on the **Unload Data** button.

6. The file download window appears. Click on **Save** to download the file.

# Loading text file to the EMP_LOAD table

You can use the **Load** page to import data from a text file into a table. Let us create a test table (EMP_TEST) to load the data exported in the preceding section:

```
CREATE TABLE emp_test AS SELECT * FROM emp WHERE 1=2;
```

To load data from the **EMP** table to a text file, follow these steps:

1. Navigate to the **Load** page (**Workspace home page** | **SQL Workshop** | **Utilities** | **Data workshop** | **Data Load** | **Text Data**).

2. Select **Existing table** for **Load Data** and **Upload file** for **Load from**. Click on the **Next** button.

3. Select the **HR** schema and click on the **Next** button.

4. Select the **EMP_TEST** table from the dropdown list and click on the **Next** button.

5. Locate the exported text file by clicking on the **Browse** button and check the **First row contains column names** checkbox. Click on the **Next** button.

6. Verify the column names and data then click on the **Load data** button to start loading into the **EMP_TEST** table.

7. APEX starts loading the data in the background. After completing the load process, APEX displays the status of loaded text data. Verify the **Succeeded** and **Failed** columns.

For this simple test, all the records should successfully get loaded into our test table. Verify the load by querying the EMP_TEST table using SQL*Plus/SQL Developer/ APEX Object Browser.

# Application Express Dashboard

The Application Express Dashboard presents a summary view of various APEX activities. Using the Dashboard, you can view the summary of a following:

- Workspace applications
- Workspace attributes and statistics
- Workspace users
- Workspace user activity
- Developer application and page changes
- Page performance
- Database objects by schema

To navigate to the dashboard go to **Application Express Home | Administration | Dashboard**. A pictorial view of the dashboard is shown in the following screenshot:

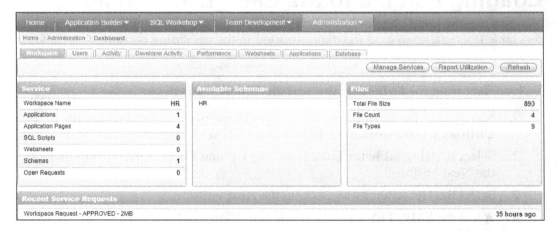

# Summary

In this chapter we used Object Browser to create database objects, the Administration component to manage Application Express users, and Application Builder to create a sample application. We have covered all the major Application Builder topics in this chapter and I hope you are now geared up to dive deeper and explore more features of Application Express.

In the next chapter, we will talk about Oracle's memory and database structure. We will discuss the types of memory available in Oracle such as **System Global Area (SGA)** and **Process Global Area (PGA)**. A database is made up of a set of files. The next chapter will guide you to understand the various types of physical files available in an Oracle database.

# References

Refer to the following Oracle documentation to learn more about Oracle Application Express:

- Application Express Administration Guide
- Application Builder User's Guide
- Application Express SQL Workshop Guide

# 8
# Managing Database and Database Storage

*A man is but the product of his thoughts what he thinks, he becomes.*
*- Mahatma Gandhi*

This chapter provides background information on memory management in Oracle Database 11*g* XE and managing physical files related to the database. Oracle memory is of two types, namely **System Global Area (SGA)** and **Process Global Area (PGA)**. SGA is a memory that is shared by all Oracle processes, while PGA is a private memory allocated to individual processes. These topics will be covered in this chapter in more detail. We will also explore the physical database structure along with the logical database structure. The topics covered in this chapter are as follows:

- Memory structure
    - System Global Area
    - Process Global Area

- Automatic Memory Management
- Important background processes
- Physical and logical database structures
    - Creating a tablespace
    - Adding datafiles to a tablespace
    - Dropping a tablespace
    - Viewing tablespace usage

- Managing Flash Recovery Area

# Memory structure

Oracle is available on almost every platform. For this reason, the physical architecture of Oracle is different on different operating systems. For example, on a Linux operating system, Oracle is implemented as multiple operating system processes whereas on Windows, Oracle is implemented as a single-threaded process.

Oracle uses memory to store information such as cached data, shared SQL and PL/SQL code, information about a session, and cursor pointers.

As mentioned earlier, Oracle memory structure is composed of two types of memory—System Global Area and Process Global Area. The following sections will cover more on these topics.

# System Global Area

**System Global Area (SGA)** is a large shared memory area that all server and background processes access. The SGA is broken into various pools as shown in the following diagram:

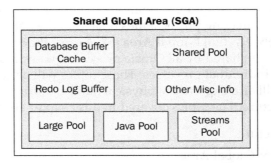

These pools are explained as follows:

- **Database buffer cache**: This is where Oracle stores database blocks before writing them to the disk and after reading them from the disk. The blocks are managed using two lists—the **Least Recently Used** (**LRU**) list and the write list. The write lists holds dirty buffers (modified buffers) that need to be written by the Database Block Writer process. The blocks in the LRU list are listed in order of use. Frequently used blocks are ranked higher than the blocks that are less frequently used. The size of the cache can be controlled using the DB_CACHE_SIZE initialization parameter.

- **Redo log buffer**: This is a circular buffer in SGA where data that needs to be written to the online redo logs is cached before it is written to the disk. The caching of redo information improves performance of the database. The LOG_BUFFER initialization parameter specifies the number of bytes allocated for the redo log buffer.

- **Shared pool**: This is one of the most critical memory structures in the SGA. It is further divided into two components — **library cache** and **dictionary cache**. The library cache stores shared SQL areas, and PL/SQL procedures and packages. The dictionary cache also known as row cache is used for storing the most recently used database objects (such as tables and indexes). The SHARED_POOL_SIZE initialization parameter is used to manually size the shared pool in the SGA.

- **Large pool**: This is an optional memory area that is configured to provide large memory allocations.

- **Java pool**: This is an optional memory area used to serve memory for all session-specific Java code and data.

- **Streams pool**: This is used to cache Oracle Streams objects. If a Streams pool is not defined, one is created automatically when Streams is first used.

The LARGE_POOL_SIZE, JAVA_POOL_SIZE, and STREAMS_POOL_SIZE initialization parameters are used to size large pool, java pool, and streams pool respectively.

# Process Global Area

**Process Global Area (PGA)** is a memory that is private to a single process and is not shared with other Oracle processes. Generally, PGA memory consists of the private SQL area, cursors, session information, and sorting area. By setting the PGA_AGGREGATE_TARGET initialization parameter, you can automatically manage the size of various work areas associated with PGA. Statistics on allocation and use of work area memory can be obtained by querying the V$PGASTAT, V$SESSTAT, and V$SQL_WORKAREA views.

# Automatic Memory Management

Oracle Database 11*g* XE uses the **Automatic Memory Management (AMM)** feature that simplifies SGA and PGA memory management significantly. The MEMORY_TARGET initialization parameter is used to automatically manage memory needs. When the MEMORY_TARGET parameter is set, Oracle Database 11*g* XE automatically sizes various memory components such as database buffer cache, Java pool, shared pool, streams pool, large pool, and process global area.

You cannot disable AMM in Oracle Database XE configuration. The MEMORY_
TARGET parameter by default is set to 1 GB when you install Oracle Database XE.
Oracle Database 11*g* XE includes four new views to support automatic memory
management:

- V$MEMORY_CURRENT_RESIZE_OPS

- V$MEMORY_DYNAMIC_COMPONENTS

- V$MEMORY_RESIZE_OPS

- V$MEMORY_TARGET_ADVICE

The amount of memory allocated to each dynamic component is displayed using the
V$MEMORY_DYNAMIC_COMPONENTS view, as shown in the following command:

```
SQL> SELECT * FROM v$memory_dynamic_components;
```

# Important background processes

There are three types of process in Oracle Database 11*g* XE:

- **Background processes**: These are the processes that start and stop
  the database. They are also responsible for writing blocks to the disk,
  maintaining the online redo log, and performing other background jobs.

- **Server processes**: These processes perform work based on the client's
  request. Tasks performed by these processes include loading data from the
  disk to SGA, modifying blocks in memory, and so on.

- **Slave processes**: These processes perform jobs on behalf of background or
  server processes.

We will look at the important background processes:

- **Database Block Writer (DBWn)**: This is responsible for writing dirty
  (modified) blocks to the disk, thus making buffer space available. More than
  one DBWn process can be configured to enhance the writing of dirty blocks
  to the disk.

- **Log Writer (LGWR)**: This is responsible for flushing the contents of the redo
  log buffer to online redo logfiles. It flushes:
  - Every three seconds
  - Whenever a COMMIT is issued
  - When the redo log buffer is one-third filled or it contains 1 MB of data

- **System Monitor (SMON)**: This is responsible for performing crash recovery.

- **Process Monitor (PMON)**: This is responsible for cleaning up after abnormally terminated connections, rollback uncommitted transactions, and release locks held.

- **Checkpoint Process (CKPT)**: This is responsible for updating the datafile header.

- **Archiver Process (ARCn)**: This is responsible for copying an online redo logfile to another location when LGWR fills up the online redo logfile. The archived redo logfiles are required to perform media recovery.

# Physical and logical database structures

A database is a collection of physical operating system files. The files that make up a database are redo logfiles, datafiles, control files, and temporary files. A logical database structure consists of tablespaces.

A **tablespace** is a logical storage unit within Oracle Database 11*g* XE. It is considered logical because a tablespace is not visible in the filesystem. A tablespace is a collection of one or more datafiles. A datafile belongs to one and only one tablespace. There are three types of tablespace in Oracle Database 11*g* XE — permanent, temporary, and undo. All our tables, indexes, and stored subprograms reside in a permanent tablespace. A temporary tablespace is used to process temporary data such as storing intermediate sorting results. All information related to undo (roll back) is stored in the undo tablespace. Undo records are used to roll back transactions when a ROLLBACK statement is issued or during recovery of the database.

Datafiles are the files that hold our tables, indexes, sequences, and other objects. Redo logfiles are transaction journals. All the transactions are recorded in these logfiles. They are used only for recovery purposes. If the database is shut down abnormally (via a shutdown abort command or due to a power failure), Oracle will use the online redo logs in order to restore the database exactly to the point where it was prior to the failure. All uncommitted transactions are rolled back.

Temporary datafiles are used to store intermediate results such as large sort operations. Temporary datafiles are not backed up by Oracle as the data residing in them is temporary.

Archived redo logfiles are copies of online redo logfiles. As online redo logfiles are reused in a circular fashion, a copy of an online redo logfile is made before it is reused. Archived redo logfiles are very crucial in recovering a database in the event of media loss and other database recovery scenarios.

- **Password file**: Oracle uses a password file to authenticate users logging in remotely as a SYS user. The password file contains the SYS password in encrypted form. The password file is automatically created when Oracle Database 11*g* XE is installed.

- **Parameter file**: There are two types of parameter files, namely PFILE and SPFILE. A PFILE is a static and editable parameter file whereas the SPFILE is a persistent binary file that can only be modified with the ALTER SYSTEM statement. The parameter file for a database is commonly known as the init.ora file. The parameter file tells the instance where the control file is and also defines other critical parameters such as SGA and PGA size, database name, and database block size.

- **Control file**: The control file is very critical to a database. It tells the instance where the datafiles and redo logfiles are residing. It also records information on checkpoints, archive logfiles. Oracle recommends multiplexing the control file on separate disks to avoid losing them in case of disk failure.

# Creating a tablespace

You can create a tablespace using the CREATE TABLESPACE command as shown in the following command:

```
SQL> CREATE TABLESPACE test_ts DATAFILE 'c:\oraclexe\app\oracle\oradata\
xe\test_ts01.dbf'
  2   SIZE 200M
  3   AUTOEXTEND ON NEXT 20M;
Tablespace created.
SQL>
```

The preceding CREATE statement creates a new tablespace called test_ts with one datafile of size 200 MB. The AUTOEXTEND ON clause specifies that the datafile is extensible when it gets full and each extension of the datafile will be of 20 MB.

# Adding datafiles to a tablespace

Datafiles can be added to a tablespace at any time. You normally add a new datafile to a tablespace when the tablespace is running out of space. You can add a datafile using the ALTER TABLESPACE command as shown in the following command:

```
SQL> ALTER TABLESPACE test_ts
  2   ADD DATAFILE 'c:\oraclexe\app\oracle\oradata\xe\test_ts02.dbf' SIZE
100M;

Tablespace altered.
SQL>
```

# Dropping a tablespace

Removing a tablespace is achieved using the DROP TABLESPACE command, shown as follows:

```
SQL> DROP TABLESPACE test_ts;


Tablespace dropped.


SQL>
```

The preceding command removes tablespace- and datafile-related information from the control file; however, the datafiles are not cleaned from the OS. To delete datafiles from the OS while you drop the tablespace run the following command:

```
SQL> DROP TABLESPACE test_ts INCLUDING CONTENTS AND DATAFILES;


Tablespace dropped.


SQL>
```

You cannot roll back the DROP TABLESPACE command so make sure that you are dropping the correct tablespace.

# Viewing the tablespace usage

The DBA_TABLESPACES, DBA_DATA_FILES, DBA_FREE_SPACE, DBA_SEGMENTS, DBA_EXTENTS, and DBA_TABLES data dictionary views are very helpful in identifying which data segment resides in what tablespace.

A query that reports the tablespace name and its usage is as follows:

```
SQL> SELECT ddf.tablespace_name,
  2          ROUND(SUM(ddf.bytes)/1024/1024) Total_mb,
  3          ROUND(SUM(ddf.bytes)/1024/1024) - dfs.Free_mb Used_mb,
  4          dfs.Free_mb
  5    FROM dba_data_files ddf,
  6         (SELECT tablespace_name,
  7                 ROUND(SUM(bytes)/1024/1024) Free_mb
  8            FROM dba_free_space
  9           GROUP BY tablespace_name) dfs
 10   WHERE dfs.tablespace_name = ddf.tablespace_name
```

```
11   GROUP BY ddf.tablespace_name, dfs.Free_mb
12   UNION ALL
13   SELECT tablespace_name,
14          ROUND(SUM(bytes_used + bytes_free)/1024/1024) Total_mb,
15          ROUND(SUM(bytes_used)/1024/1024) Used_mb,
16          ROUND(SUM(bytes_free)/1024/1024) Free_mb
17   FROM V$temp_space_header
18   GROUP BY tablespace_name;
```

| TABLESPACE_NAME | TOTAL_MB | USED_MB | FREE_MB |
|-----------------|---------:|--------:|--------:|
| SYSAUX          |      670 |     635 |      35 |
| SYSTEM          |      390 |     360 |      30 |
| TEST_TS         |      200 |       1 |     199 |
| USERS           |      100 |       5 |      95 |
| UNDOTBS1        |       25 |      10 |      15 |
| TEMP            |       20 |      15 |       5 |

```
6 rows selected.
SQL>
```

You can also use Oracle Database XE GUI to monitor the storage usage. On Windows, you can navigate to **Start | All Programs | Oracle Database 11g Express Edition | Get Started**. Click on the **Storage** link and enter the SYS user credentials and you will be presented with the following screen:

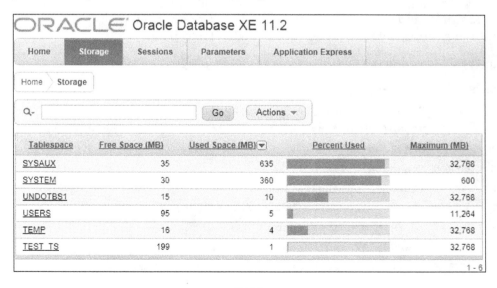

# Managing the Flash Recovery Area

Oracle Database 11*g* XE stores database backups, redo logfiles, and archive redo logfiles in **Flash Recovery Area (FRA)**. Optionally you can place a member of the multiplexed control file in FRA. The V$RECOVERY_FILE_DEST view provides details of FRA location and usage. Run the following query to determine the FRA details:

```
SQL> set line 100
SQL> column name format a45
SQL>
SQL> SELECT name,
  2   ROUND(space_limit/1024/1024) space_limit,
  3   ROUND(space_used/1024/1024) space_used,
  4   ROUND(space_reclaimable/1024/1024) space_reclaimable
  5   FROM v$recovery_file_dest;


NAME                                     SPACE_LIMIT   SPACE_USED SPACE_RECLAIMABLE
---------------------------------------------   ----------- ---------- ----
------------
C:\oraclexe\app\oracle\
fast_recovery_area                       10240         100               0
SQL>
```

Using the DB_RECOVERY_FILE_DEST and DB_RECOVERY_FILE_DEST_SIZE initialization parameters we can define the FRA location and size. To set the flash recovery area to 50 GB, enter the following commands:

```
SQL> ALTER SYSTEM SET db_recovery_file_dest_size=50G SCOPE=both;
System altered.
SQL>
```

```
While configuring FRA, make sure that you set the size (db_recovery_file_
dest_size ) first and then the location (db_recovery_file_dest).
```

```
V$FLASH_RECOVERY_AREA_USAGE is another useful view that provides space
usage information based on file types (control files, redo logfiles etc)
```

To disable the flash recovery area, set the DB_RECOVERY_FILE_DEST initialization parameter to a null string as shown below:

```
SQL> ALTER SYSTEM SET db_recovery_file_dest= '' SCOPE=both;
```

# Summary

In this chapter we explored all the components that make up an SGA. Also, we learned about the PGA. We also explored the important types of files that make an Oracle database such as the parameter file, password file, control file, datafile, and redo logfiles. We reviewed how to create and manage tablespaces and control the Flash Recovery Area.

The next chapter is dedicated to data loading and unloading. In this chapter, we will discuss different methods and options available within Oracle Database to load and unload the data using the Oracle proprietary tools.

# 9

# Moving Data between Oracle Databases

*Pleasure in the job puts perfection in the work. - Aristotle*

This chapter describes how to move data from Oracle Database 10*g* Express Edition to Oracle Database 11*g* Edition using Oracle's Export/Import utilities. Oracle Database XE supports traditional Export/Import utilities and Data Pump Export/Import utilities. This chapter discusses these approaches in more detail, covering the following topics:

- Exporting and importing data
- Traditional Export/Import (`exp`/`imp`) utilities
- Data Pump Export/Import (`expdp`/`impdp`) utilities
- Moving data between Oracle Database 10*g* XE and Oracle Database 11*g* XE

## Exporting and importing data

Oracle's Export and Import utilities are used to move the data between different machines, databases, and schema. When exporting, database objects are dumped into a proprietary binary file. This binary file is then used to import database objects into another Oracle database.

Oracle's Export and Import utilities are also used to perform logical database backup and recovery.

# Traditional Export and Import (exp/imp) utilities

The traditional Export and Import utilities provide a simple way to move your data between Oracle databases. The Export utility extracts data from the database and generates a binary file as the output file. We can then import data into the destination database using this binary file.

The Export and Import utilities are invoked using the `exp` and `imp` commands respectively. These utilities can be used to move data between Oracle databases even if they reside on different platforms (hardware and software configurations).

The Export and Import utilities support the following modes:

- **Full mode**: Exports and imports a full database.
- **Tablespace mode**: Using this mode we can move one or more tablespaces from one Oracle database to another. The transportable tablespaces can be exported in Oracle Database XE but can only be imported in an Enterprise Edition.
- **User mode**: In this mode, we can export and import all objects owned by a particular user.
- **Table mode**: In this mode, we can export and import specific tables.

Examples of using the Export utility in different modes are as follows:

```
-- Export full database
exp system/******** FULL=y FILE=c:\fulldb_exp.dmp LOG= c:\fulldb_exp.
log
-- Export a User by connecting to the database with DBA privilege
exp system/******** OWNER=hr FILE=c:\hr_exp.dmp LOG=c:\hr_exp.log
-- Export a User itself
exp hr/******** file=c:\hr_exp.dmp log=c:\hr_exp.log
-- Export a table
exp hr/******** TABLES=employees FILE=c:\hr_employees_exp.dmp LOG= c:\
hr_employees_exp.log
```

Examples of using the Import utility in different modes are as follows:

```
-- Import Full database
imp system/sys1234 FULL=Y FILE=c:\fulldb_exp.dmp LOG=c:\fulldb_imp.log"
-- Import schema
imp system/sys1234 FROMUSER=hr TOUSER=test FILE=c:\hr_exp.dmp LOG=c:\
hr_imp.log
-- Import a table
imp hr/******** FROMUSER=hr TOUSER=test FILE=c:\hr_employees_exp.dmp
LOG=c:\hr_employees_imp.log
```

# Data Pump Export/Import (expdp/impdp) utilities

The Data Pump Export and Import utilities were first introduced in Oracle Database 10*g*. Data Pump enables high speed data and metadata transfers. The Data Pump Export and Import utilities are invoked using the `expdp` and `impdp` commands respectively. Data Pump is similar to traditional export and import utilities but it has many advantages, some of which are as follows:

- Ability to estimate job times
- Ability to estimate the space required by the export dump file without actually exporting the data
- Remapping capabilities
- Ability to restart failed jobs
- Monitor running jobs

Data Pump is server-based, meaning dump files and logfiles are accessed relative to the database server-based directory paths. We need to create a directory object specifying to the OS directory path before using data pump utilities. An Oracle directory object maps a name to a directory on the OS filesystem. Once the directory is created, the user creating the directory object needs to grant the READ or WRITE privilege on the directory object to other database users.

For example, the following SQL statement creates a database directory object (exp_dir) that is mapped to an OS directory (`c:\oraclexe\exp_dumps`):

```
SQL> CREATE OR REPLACE DIRECTORY exp_dir AS 'c:\oraclexe\exp_dumps';
SQL> GRANT READ, WRITE ON DIRECTORY exp_dir TO hr;
```

Examples of using Data Pump Export/Import utilities in different modes are as follows:

```
-- Export full database
expdp system/******** FULL=y DIRECTORY=exp_dir DUMPFILE=fulldb_exp.dmp
LOGFILE=fulldb_exp.log
-- Export a schema
expdp hr/******** SCHEMAS=hr DIRECTORY=exp_dir DUMPFILE=hr_expdp.dmp
LOGFILE=hr_expdp.log
-- Export a table
expdp hr/******** TABLES=employees DIRECTORY=exp_dir DUMPFILE=emp_
expdp.dmp LOGFILE=emp_expdp.log

-- Import Full database
impdp system/******** FULL=y DIRECTORY=exp_dir DUMPFILE=fulldb_exp.dmp
LOGFILE=fulldb_imp.log
```

```
-- Import schema
impdp hr/******** SCHEMAS=hr DIRECTORY=exp_dir DUMPFILE=hr_expdp.dmp
LOGFILE=hr_impdp.log
-- Import a table
impdp hr/******** TABLES=employees DIRECTORY=exp_dir DUMPFILE=emp_
expdp.dmp LOGFILE=emp_impdp.log
```

The EXCLUDE and INCLUDE parameters available in Data Pump export/import are used as metadata filters. Using these parameters you can Exclude/Include database objects. Using the EXCLUDE parameter, you can specify database objects and object types that you want to exclude from the export operation. Similarly, using the INCLUDE parameter, you specify database objects and object types for the current export mode.

An example of exporting all objects belonging to the HR schema excluding the DEPARTMENTS table is as follows:

```
expdp system/sys SCHEMAS=hr EXCLUDE=TABLE:\'IN (\'DEPARTMENTS\')\'
DIRECTORY= exp_dir DUMPFILE=hr_no_dept_expdp.dmp LOGFILE= hr_no_dept_
expdp.log
```

# Moving data between Oracle Database 10*g* XE and Oracle Database 11*g* XE

Follow the guidelines presented in this section if you want to do either of the following:

- Move data between Oracle Database 10*g* XE and Oracle Database 11*g* XE
- Upgrade your Oracle Database 10*g* XE to Oracle Database 11*g* XE

The steps are as follows:

1. Create a database directory object by connecting to Oracle Database 10*g* XE as SYS user:

   ```
   SQL> CREATE OR REPLACE DIRECTORY dump_dir AS 'c:\xetest';

   SQL> GRANT READ,WRITE ON DIRECTORY dump_dir TO system;
   ```

2. Export the data from Oracle Database 10*g* XE:

   ```
   expdp system/******** full=Y EXCLUDE=SCHEMA:\'LIKE
   \'APEX_%\'\',SCHEMA:\'LIKE \'FLOWS_%\'\' directory=DUMP_DIR
   dumpfile=DB10G.dmp logfile=DB10G_expdp.log
   expdp system/******** TABLES=FLOWS_FILES.WWV_FLOW_FILE_OBJECTS$
   directory=DUMP_DIR dumpfile=DB10G2.dmp logfile=DB10G_expdp.log
   ```

3. Uninstall Oracle Database 10*g* XE.

4. Install Oracle Database 11*g* XE.

5. Create a database directory object by connecting as SYS user:

```
SQL> CREATE OR REPLACE DIRECTORY dump_dir AS 'c:\xetest';
SQL> GRANT READ, WRITE ON DIRECTORY dump_dir TO system;
```

6. Import data exported from Oracle Database 10g XE into Oracle Database 11*g* XE:

```
impdp system/sys1234 full=Y directory=DUMP_DIR dumpfile=DB10G.dmp
logfile=DB10G_impdp.log
impdp system/sys1234 directory=DUMP_DIR TABLE_EXISTS_ACTION=APPEND
TABLES=FLOWS_FILES.WWV_FLOW_FILE_OBJECTS$ dumpfile=DB10G2.dmp
logfile=DB10G_impdp.log
```

# Exporting data using SQL Developer

Exporting data and metadata using SQL Developer is very simple. From the menu go to **Tools | Data Export**. This launches the **Data Export** wizard. You may choose to export both the metadata and data, or either of the two. It's pretty straightforward from the interface.

You should choose an appropriate method to import metadata or data depending on how the object was exported.

# Summary

In this chapter we explored Oracle database utilities such as traditional Export/Import and Data Pump Export/Import to load and unload data from an Oracle database. We also learned to move data between Oracle Database 10*g* Express Edition and Oracle Database 11*g* Express Edition.

The next chapter will talk about database migration. We will learn to migrate our XE database to other database editions. The chapter provides step-by-step instructions on migrating from XE to Enterprise Edition.

# 10
# Upgrading Oracle Database 11*g* XE to Other Database Editions

*Indeed, an ignorant man who is generous is dearer to God than a worshipper who is miserly. - Prophet Muhammed*

In this chapter we will learn how to upgrade Oracle Database 11*g* XE to other database editions. Oracle Database 11*g* XE offers upgrade as you go. Oracle grows with your needs, offering a smooth upgrade path.

## Upgrading Oracle Database 11*g* XE to Oracle Database 11*g* Enterprise Edition

This section provides a step-by-step guide on upgrading Oracle Database 11*g* XE to Oracle Database 11*g* Enterprise Edition. Ensure that the release number and patch level of Enterprise Edition server software are the same as the original Express Edition server software. For example, if the Express Edition is 11.2.0.2, then your Enterprise Edition should also be 11.2.0.2.

The following are the steps to upgrade Oracle Database 11*g* XE (11.2.0.2) to Oracle Database 11*g* Enterprise Edition on a Windows environment:

1. Shut down the database.
2. Stop Windows service (this step is not required under Linux).

3. Back up the database. You may use one of the following three backup methods to safeguard your database before starting the upgrade process:

   ° Oracle's export utility (discussed in the previous chapter). If you choose to use this method, it should be performed before shutting down the database.

   ° RMAN Backup (discussed in the next chapter). This step should also be performed before shutting down the database.

   ° Shut down the database and use the OS copy command to copy database files to a backup location.

4. Create a new parent folder — `C:\app\oracle`. This directory will host our new database-related files (control files, data files, redo log files, and so on).

5. Copy all the directories from `C:\oraclexe\app\oracle` to the `C:\app\oracle` location except the `product` folder. This will copy our database-related files and diagnostic files to the new location.

6. Copy the following configuration files to a temporary folder (`C:\database`):

   ° Backup files — `initXE.ora` and `PWDXE.ora` found under the `C:\oraclexe\app\oracle\product\11.2.0\server\database` directory.

   ° Backup file — `SPFILEXE.ora` located in `C:\oraclexe\app\oracle\product\11.2.0\server\dbs`.

7. Create a `pfile` using the following command. This is required as we would make changes to important initialization parameters:

```
SQL> create pfile='c:\xe.ora' from spfile;
File created.
SQL>
```

8. Uninstall Oracle Database 11g XE from your machine.

9. Install Oracle Database 11g Enterprise Edition software only.

10. Copy the password file from the backup location (`C:\database`) to the new Oracle home — `$ORACLE_HOME\dbs`.

11. Open `C:\XE.ora` in Notepad, and replace `C:\oraclexe\app\oracle` with `C:\app\oracle` and save the initialization parameter file.

12. Create a new `spfile` as follows:

```
SQL> create spfile from pfile='c:\xe.ora';
File created.
SQL>
```

13. Start the database in mount mode:

```
SQL> startup nomount
ORACLE instance started.

Total System Global Area  644468736 bytes
Fixed Size                  1385480 bytes
Variable Size             255855608 bytes
Database Buffers          381681664 bytes
Redo Buffers                5545984 bytes
Database mounted.
SQL>
```

14. Make a note of the data file, temporary file, and redo log file's location by querying the V$DATAFILE, V$TEMPFILE, and V$LOGFILE views respectively:

```
SQL> select name from v$datafile;

NAME
--------------------------------------------------
C:\ORACLEXE\APP\ORACLE\ORADATA\XE\SYSTEM.DBF
C:\ORACLEXE\APP\ORACLE\ORADATA\XE\UNDOTBS1.DBF
C:\ORACLEXE\APP\ORACLE\ORADATA\XE\SYSAUX.DBF
C:\ORACLEXE\APP\ORACLE\ORADATA\XE\USERS.DBF

SQL>

SQL> select member from v$logfile;

MEMBER
-----------------------------------------------------------------
C:\ORACLEXE\APP\ORACLE\FAST_RECOVERY_AREA\XE\ONLINELOG\O1_
MF_2_7K7QDGXN_.
        LOG
C:\ORACLEXE\APP\ORACLE\FAST_RECOVERY_AREA\XE\ONLINELOG\O1_
MF_1_7K7QDCYN_.
        LOG

SQL>

SQL> select name from v$tempfile;

NAME
--------------------------------------------------
C:\ORACLEXE\APP\ORACLE\ORADATA\XE\TEMP.DBF

SQL>
```

15. Rename the data file locations using the ALTER DATABASE RENAME FILE statement:

```
SQL> alter database rename file
        'C:\ORACLEXE\APP\ORACLE\ORADATA\XE\SYSTEM.DBF' to
   2  'C:\app\oracle\oradata\XE\SYSTEM.DBF';

Database altered.

SQL>
SQL> alter database rename file
        'C:\ORACLEXE\APP\ORACLE\ORADATA\XE\UNDOTBS1.DBF' to
   2  'C:\app\oracle\oradata\XE\UNDOTBS1.DBF';

Database altered.

SQL>
SQL> alter database rename file
        'C:\ORACLEXE\APP\ORACLE\ORADATA\XE\SYSAUX.DBF' to
   2  'C:\app\oracle\oradata\XE\SYSAUX.DBF';

Database altered.

SQL>
SQL> alter database rename file
        'C:\ORACLEXE\APP\ORACLE\ORADATA\XE\USERS.DBF' to
   2  'C:\app\oracle\oradata\XE\USERS.DBF';

Database altered.

SQL>
```

16. Rename the temporary files:

```
SQL> alter database rename file
        'C:\ORACLEXE\APP\ORACLE\ORADATA\XE\TEMP.DBF' to
   2  'C:\app\oracle\oradata\XE\TEMP.DBF';

Database altered.

SQL>
```

17. Similarly, rename the redo log files:

```
SQL> alter database rename file
   2  'C:\ORACLEXE\APP\ORACLE\FAST_RECOVERY_AREA
        \XE\ONLINELOG\O1_MF_2_7K7QDGXN_.LOG' to
   3  'C:\app\oracle\fast_recovery_area
        \XE\ONLINELOG\O1_MF_2_7K7QDGXN_.LOG';
```

```
Database altered.

SQL> alter database rename file
  2  'C:\ORACLEXE\APP\ORACLE\FAST_RECOVERY_AREA
        \XE\ONLINELOG\O1_MF_1_7K7QDCYN_.LOG' to
  3  'C:\app\oracle\fast_recovery_area
        \XE\ONLINELOG\O1_MF_1_7K7QDCYN_.LOG';

Database altered.

SQL>
```

18. Open the database:

```
SQL> alter database open;

Database altered.

SQL>
```

19. Optionally, run the `catalog.sql` and `catproc.sql` scripts as follows:

```
SQL> @?\rdbms\admin\catalog.sql

SQL> @?\rdbms\admin\catproc.sql
```

It's better to execute the preceding two scripts because of the complexity of data dictionary and to be sure that all the Enterprise Edition objects are created.

Your database is now using the Oracle Database 11*g* Enterprise Edition version of the software. Using the preceding procedure, you can upgrade Express Edition to Standard Edition or Standard Edition One.

# Summary

In this chapter we have taken a detailed step-by-step approach for upgrading Express Edition to Enterprise Edition.

The next chapter is dedicated to backup and recovery. Backup and recovery are of high significance, as we should always protect our databases from data loss caused by a variety of failures. We will discuss various backup and recovery techniques in the next chapter.

# 11
# Backup and Recovery

*There are a thousand excuses for failure but never a good reason. - Mark Twain*

In this chapter we will discuss the basics of Oracle Database XE backup and recovery. This chapter introduces Oracle's backup and recovery tool, **Recovery Manager (RMAN)**. We will also discuss a few backup and recovery scenarios. The following are the topics covered in this chapter:

- A brief introduction to backup and recovery
- Recovery Manager
- Connecting to Oracle Database XE using RMAN
- The ARCHIVELOG mode
- Placing a database in the ARCHIVELOG mode
- Backing up a database (the NOARCHIVELOG mode)
- Simulating a database failure (the NOARCHIVELOG mode)
- Restoring the NOARCHIVELOG database
- Configuring the RMAN environment
- Backing up the ARCHIVELOG database
- Simulating a database failure (the ARCHIVELOG mode)
- Restoring ARCHIVELOG database

The full range of backup and recovery techniques is out of the scope of this book. Refer to Oracle documentation for more details.

# Introduction to backup and recovery

In information technology, a backup or the process of backing up is making copies of data, which may be used to restore the original after a data loss event (refer to the Backup definition at Wikipedia). Recovering of database is a process a reconstructing the database after data loss.

# Recovery Manager

**Recovery Manager** (**RMAN**) is Oracle's command-line utility for backing up and recovering an Oracle database. RMAN is fully integrated with Oracle database and is Oracle's recommended tool for backing up and recovering Oracle databases. RMAN is installed automatically with the database.

# Connecting to Oracle Database XE using RMAN

Start the RMAN executable (RMAN.exe) in the command prompt of your operating system. A RMAN prompt will appear on your screen. Now you can connect to your database using the SYSDBA privilege account as follows:

```
-- connect to the database
RMAN> connect target /

connected to target database: XE (DBID=2655045848)

RMAN> exit
```

Alternatively, you can connect to the database when you start the RMAN client session as follows:

```
-- start RMAN client and connect to the target database

C:\oraclexe\app\oracle\product\11.2.0\server\bin>rman target /

Recovery Manager: Release 11.2.0.2.0 - Production on Wed Apr 4
14:38:53 2012

Copyright (c) 1982, 2009, Oracle and/or its affiliates.  All rights
reserved.

connected to target database: XE (DBID=2655045848)

RMAN>
```

# The ARCHIVELOG mode

Databases can be run in one of two modes—the ARCHIVELOG mode or the NOARCHVIELOG mode. In NOARCHVIELOG mode, the redo log files are reused by the Oracle database engine without being copied to an offline location. In ARCHIVELOG mode, Oracle copies the filled online redo log files to one or more offline locations before they are reused. These redo log files, which are saved offline, are called **archived redo log files**. The ARCH process is responsible for archiving when automatic archiving is enabled. You use the archived redo log files to recover a database and update a standby database.

The ARCHIVELOG mode is very important for mission-critical production databases. Databases can be backed up in the open mode when running in the ARCHIVELOG mode. Also, the ARCHIVELOG mode provides point-in-time recovery. It is generally not necessary for test and development databases.

# Placing a database in the ARCHIVELOG mode

To place a database in the ARCHIVELOG mode, perform the following steps:

1. Create a directory to store archived redo log files.

2. Update the log_archive_dest_1 initialization parameter to point to the archived redo log file location:

   ```
   SQL> ALTER SYSTEM SET log_archive_dest_1='LOCATION=C:\oraclexe\
   app\oracle\fast_recovery_area\XE\ARCHIVELOG' SCOPE=both;
   ```

3. Start the database in MOUNT mode:

   ```
   SQL> STARTUP MOUNT
   ```

4. Place the database in ARCHIVELOG mode:

   ```
   SQL> ALTER DATABASE ARCHIVELOG;
   ```

5. Open the database:

   ```
   SQL> ALTER DATABASE OPEN;
   ```

6. To disable the ARCHIVELOG mode of the database, you would do the following:

   ° Start the database in MOUNT mode.

   ° Disable the ARCHIVELOG mode:

     ```
     SQL> alter database noarchivelog;
     ```

   ° Start the database in open mode:

     ```
     SQL> alter database open;
     ```

# Backing up a database (the NOARCHIVELOG mode)

You can manually take a backup using the BACKUP command in RMAN or use the Oracle Database XE-supplied script. In this section we will use the Oracle Database XE-supplied script to perform a full database backup. Remember, RMAN by default creates backups to disk.

Backing up a database in the NOARCHIVELOG mode requires the database to be in a MOUNT state. This backup is called a **consistent backup**. When a consistent backup is restored, there is no need to perform any recovery.

Start the backup by running the Oracle Database XE-supplied backup script, located under **Startup | Oracle Database 11g Express Edition | Backup Database** on a Windows machine, and by executing $ORACLE_HOME/config/scripts/backup.sh on a Linux environment. The backup script does the following:

- Shuts down the database
- Starts the database in MOUNT mode
- Performs backup
- Opens the database for read/write operations

The following screenshot shows RMAN backup in progress on a Windows environment:

Now let us check our backup pieces within RMAN, as shown in the following screenshot:

```
RMAN> list backup;

List of Backup Sets
===================

BS Key  Type LU Size       Device Type Elapsed Time Completion Time
------- ---- -- ---------- ----------- ------------ ---------------
11      Full    824.39M    DISK        00:00:58     04-APR-12
        BP Key: 11   Status: AVAILABLE  Compressed: NO   Tag: TAG20120404T151611
        Piece Name: C:\ORACLEXE\APP\ORACLE\FAST_RECOVERY_AREA\XE\BACKUPSET\2012_04_04\01_MF_NNNDF_TA
G20120404T151611_7QRGWDU2_.BKP
   List of Datafiles in backup set 11
   File LU Type Ckp SCN   Ckp Time   Name
   ---- -- ---- --------- ---------- ----
   1       Full 573620    04-APR-12  C:\ORACLEXE\APP\ORACLE\ORADATA\XE\SYSTEM.DBF
   2       Full 573620    04-APR-12  C:\ORACLEXE\APP\ORACLE\ORADATA\XE\UNDOTBS1.DBF
   3       Full 573620    04-APR-12  C:\ORACLEXE\APP\ORACLE\ORADATA\XE\SYSAUX.DBF
   4       Full 573620    04-APR-12  C:\ORACLEXE\APP\ORACLE\ORADATA\XE\USERS.DBF

BS Key  Type LU Size       Device Type Elapsed Time Completion Time
------- ---- -- ---------- ----------- ------------ ---------------
12      Full    9.36M      DISK        00:00:02     04-APR-12
        BP Key: 12   Status: AVAILABLE  Compressed: NO   Tag: TAG20120404T151718
        Piece Name: C:\ORACLEXE\APP\ORACLE\FAST_RECOVERY_AREA\XE\AUTOBACKUP\2012_04_04\01_MF_S_77972
8539_7QRGYHQ7_.BKP
   SPFILE Included: Modification time: 04-APR-12
   SPFILE db_unique_name: XE
   Control File Included: Ckp SCN: 573620       Ckp time: 04-APR-12

RMAN>
```

In the preceding screenshot, you can see that all the database files that belong to our database have been backed up. RMAN groups one or more datafiles into a backup piece, and one or more backup pieces are grouped together and are called a **backup set**.

# Simulating a database failure (the NOARCHIVELOG mode)

Now that we have a valid backup in place, let us simulate a database failure. Let us use the **hr_test** table created earlier in this book for our test. We have five records in the **hr_test** table, as shown in the following screenshot:

```
SQL> select * from hr.hr_test;

    EMP_NO EMP_NAME                      DATE_OF_B    SALARY
---------- ----------------------------- --------- ---------
         1 Allen Solly                   05-JAN-80       500
         4 Tom Green                     01-FEB-82        80
         5 King Lucifer                  01-JUN-83      1000
         2 Ricky Blake                   01-DEC-75       600
         3 Karty Sheen                   06-MAR-85       700

SQL>
SQL>
```

For this test, we will perform the following steps to simulate a database failure:

1.  Take a full database backup.

2.  Insert a record in the **hr_test** table. (Any changes to the database after the backup will be lost once we restore the database. So, we will lose this record in the recovery process.)

3.  Insert the following line of code into **hr_test**:

    ```
    VALUES (6, 'test record', sysdate, 100);
    Shutdown database
    ```

4.  Rename datafiles folder — ORADATA/XE to ORADATA/XE-BACKUP.

5.  Create a new empty folder — XE.

6.  Start the database now. (Oracle instance starts up in NOMOUNT mode and fails to mount the database, as Oracle is not able to find the control file while mounting the database.)

# Restoring the NOARCHIVELOG database

Restoring a backup is a process of bringing the database back to a state before crash. As our database is in the NOARCHIVELOG mode, all changes made after the backup will be lost. We will be able to restore the database to the last backup.

We can restore the database either by using the Oracle Database XE-supplied restore script or by manually entering the restore commands in RMAN command prompt. In this section we will use the Oracle Database XE-supplied script to restore the database.

Start the restore by running the Oracle Database XE-supplied restore script, located under **Startup | Oracle Database 11g Express Edition | Restore Database** on the Window environment, and by executing $ORACLE_HOME/config/scripts/ restore.sh on Linux. The restore script does the following:

*   Restores spfile and controlfile from autobackup
*   Restarts the database in MOUNT mode
*   Restores the database
*   Opens the database with the RESETLOGS option

The following screenshot shows the RMAN restore process in progress:

Once the RMAN restore procedure completes, our database is ready to use. Log in to the database and query the hr_test table for the number of records. You will not find the last inserted test record in the table, because this record did not exist when the backup was taken.

# Configuring the RMAN environment

We can use the SHOW ALL command to display the current values of RMAN-configured settings for our target database. The following are a few of the values we can configure:

- Database retention policy
- Default device type for backup
- Control file automatic backup
- Enable/disable database encryption

Let us configure automatic backup of controlfile as follows:

This setting will enable the database to take an autobackup of `controlfile` whenever a database backup occurs or the database structure metadata (add/drop of datafiles/ tablespaces) in `controlfile` changes.

For more information on other parameters, refer to *Oracle Database Backup and Recovery User's Guide*.

# Backing up the ARCHIVELOG database

Let us first place the database in the ARCHIVELOG mode before backing up the database. We have already gone through the procedure of placing the database in the ARCHIVELOG mode earlier in this chapter.

```
SQL> alter system set log_archive_dest_1 = 'LOCATION=C:\oraclexe\app\oracle\fast_recovery_area\XE\AR
CHIVELOG' scope=both;

System altered.

SQL>
SQL> shutdown immediate
Database closed.
Database dismounted.
ORACLE instance shut down.
SQL>
SQL> startup mount
ORACLE instance started.

Total System Global Area   644468736 bytes
Fixed Size                   1385488 bytes
Variable Size              239078384 bytes
Database Buffers           398458880 bytes
Redo Buffers                 5545984 bytes
Database mounted.
SQL>
SQL> alter database archivelog;

Database altered.

SQL> alter database open;

Database altered.

SQL> archive log list
Database log mode              Archive Mode
Automatic archival             Enabled
Archive destination            C:\oraclexe\app\oracle\fast_recovery_area\XE\ARCHIVELOG
Oldest online log sequence     1
Next log sequence to archive   1
Current log sequence           1
SQL>
```

Switch a few log files after opening the database using ALTER SYSTEM SWITCH LOGFILE and look for new archived redo log files in the `C:\oraclexe\app\oracle\ fast_recovery_area\XE\ARCHIVELOG\` folder.

Now our database is ready for the backup. Let us now take a manual backup instead of using the Oracle Database XE-supplied backup script. Log in to the RMAN session, connect to the target database, and run the backup command.

The following is the simple backup command that we will use to back up our database:

```
-- RMAN back command to backup database and archive logs
RMAN> backup database plus archivelog;
```

Alternatively, you can specify the backup location using the FORMAT clause. %U
generates unique filenames for the backup pieces as follows:

```
RMAN> backup database plus archivelog format 'c:\xe\backup_%U';
```

The preceding command does the following:

- Creates a folder under the flash recovery area
- Automatically backs up spfile and controlfile
- Backs up the entire database
- Finally, backs up all the archive log files

The following screenshot shows the backup process:

Now that we have successfully backed up our database, let us query RMAN to get the backup details. I am listing the backups in summary mode as the verbose mode would generate too much output. However, you may check the verbose on your computers.

```
RMAN> list backup summary;

List of Backups
===============
Key    TY LV S Device Type Completion Time #Pieces #Copies Compressed Tag
----   -- -- - ----------- --------------- ------- ------- ---------- ---
9      B  A  A DISK        07-APR-12       1       1       NO         TAG20120407T003022
10     B  F  A DISK        07-APR-12       1       1       NO         TAG20120407T003023
11     B  F  A DISK        07-APR-12       1       1       NO         TAG20120407T003023
12     B  A  A DISK        07-APR-12       1       1       NO         TAG20120407T003124

RMAN>
```

# Simulating a database failure (the ARCHIVELOG mode)

Now it's time to start playing with our database. We have recovered our database (NOARCHIVELOG) from a simulated database failure earlier in this chapter. We will repeat a similar approach with our database in the ARCHIVELOG mode.

For this test we will be performing the following steps to simulate a database failure:

1.  Take a full database backup.

2.  Insert a record in the hr_test table:

    ```
    SQL>INSERT into hr_test VALUES (6, 'test record', sysdate, 100);
    SQL> COMMIT;
    ```

3.  Switch the archive logs:

    ```
    SQL> ALTER SYSTEM SWITCH LOGFILE;
    ```

4.  Back up the archive logs:

    ```
    RMAN> backup archivelog all;
    ```

5.  Shut down the database.

6.  Rename the datafiles folder — ORADATA/XE to ORADATA/XE-ARCH-BACKUP.

7.  Create a new empty folder — XE.

8.  Start the database now. (Oracle instance starts up in NOMOUNT mode and fails to mount the database, as Oracle is not able to find controlfile while mounting the database.)

# Restoring the ARCHIVELOG database

The steps involved in recovering an ARCHIVELOG mode database differ from that of the NOARCHIVELOG mode database. The steps involved are as follows:

1. Start the database instance in the NOMOUNT mode.

2. Restore the controlfile.

3. Mount the database.

4. Restore the database.

5. Recover the database.

6. Open the database.

7. Query the hr_test table to confirm the change.

Start the database instance in the NOMOUNT mode using either SQL*Plus or the RMAN client. The next step in the process is to restore controlfile and mount the database. Restore controlfile from the autobackup, as shown in the following screenshot:

```
RMAN> restore controlfile from autobackup;

Starting restore at 08-APR-12
allocated channel: ORA_DISK_1
channel ORA_DISK_1: SID=10 device type=DISK

recovery area destination: C:\oraclexe\app\oracle\fast_recovery_area
database name (or database unique name) used for search: XE
channel ORA_DISK_1: AUTOBACKUP C:\ORACLEXE\APP\ORACLE\FAST_RECOVERY_AREA\XE\AUTOBACKUP\2012_04_08\01
_MF_S_780074967_7R3158LT_.BKP found in the recovery area
channel ORA_DISK_1: looking for AUTOBACKUP on day: 20120408
channel ORA_DISK_1: restoring control file from AUTOBACKUP C:\ORACLEXE\APP\ORACLE\FAST_RECOVERY_AREA
\XE\AUTOBACKUP\2012_04_08\01_MF_S_780074967_7R3158LT_.BKP
channel ORA_DISK_1: control file restore from AUTOBACKUP complete
output file name=C:\ORACLEXE\APP\ORACLE\ORADATA\XE\CONTROL.DBF
Finished restore at 08-APR-12

RMAN>
```

RMAN searches for a backup of controlfile in the default location, and once located, RMAN restores controlfile to its default location. Now mount the database using the ALTER DATABASE MOUNT command.

The database is now mounted and it is the time to restore the database. The control file has all the information of the backup and when we restore the database, it will read the appropriate backup file and restore the datafiles to their default locations. Restore is a process of copying datafiles from backup location to disk.

The following screenshot shows the **restore database** command:

The next step after restoring the database is to perform database recovery. Recovery is the process of applying redo logs to the database to roll it forward. The following screenshot shows the **recover database** command:

```
RMAN> recover database;

Starting recover at 08-APR-12
using channel ORA_DISK_1

starting media recovery

archived log for thread 1 with sequence 2 is already on disk as file C:\ORACLEXE\APP\ORACLE\FAST_REC
OVERY_AREA\XE\ARCHIVELOGARC0000000002_0780064622.0001
archived log for thread 1 with sequence 3 is already on disk as file C:\ORACLEXE\APP\ORACLE\FAST_REC
OVERY_AREA\XE\ARCHIVELOGARC0000000003_0780064622.0001
archived log for thread 1 with sequence 4 is already on disk as file C:\ORACLEXE\APP\ORACLE\FAST_REC
OVERY_AREA\XE\ARCHIVELOGARC0000000004_0780064622.0001
archived log for thread 1 with sequence 5 is already on disk as file C:\ORACLEXE\APP\ORACLE\FAST_REC
OVERY_AREA\XE\ONLINELOG\O1_MF_1_7QYQOGJZ_.LOG
archived log for thread 1 with sequence 6 is already on disk as file C:\ORACLEXE\APP\ORACLE\FAST_REC
OVERY_AREA\XE\ONLINELOG\O1_MF_2_7QYQOHKM_.LOG
archived log file name=C:\ORACLEXE\APP\ORACLE\FAST_RECOVERY_AREA\XE\ARCHIVELOGARC0000000002_07800646
22.0001 thread=1 sequence=2
archived log file name=C:\ORACLEXE\APP\ORACLE\FAST_RECOVERY_AREA\XE\ARCHIVELOGARC0000000003_07800646
22.0001 thread=1 sequence=3
archived log file name=C:\ORACLEXE\APP\ORACLE\FAST_RECOVERY_AREA\XE\ARCHIVELOGARC0000000004_07800646
22.0001 thread=1 sequence=4
archived log file name=C:\ORACLEXE\APP\ORACLE\FAST_RECOVERY_AREA\XE\ONLINELOG\O1_MF_1_7QYQOGJZ_.LOG
thread=1 sequence=5
archived log file name=C:\ORACLEXE\APP\ORACLE\FAST_RECOVERY_AREA\XE\ONLINELOG\O1_MF_2_7QYQOHKM_.LOG
thread=1 sequence=6
media recovery complete, elapsed time: 00:00:04
Finished recover at 08-APR-12

RMAN>
```

The **recover database** command applies all archived redo log files and brings the database to the last consistent state. After successfully recovering the database, it's time to open the database. We open the database with the **resetlogs** option, as shown in the following screenshot:

```
RMAN> alter database open resetlogs;
database opened
RMAN>
```

Now that we have successfully restored and recovered the database, it's time to query the **hr_test** table and check for our test record:

```
SQL> select * from hr.hr_test;

    EMP_NO EMP_NAME                         DATE_OF_B     SALARY
---------- -------------------------------- ------------ ----------
         6 test                             08-APR-12        100
         1 Allen Solly                      05-JAN-80        500
         4 Tom Green                        01-FEB-82         80
         5 King Lucifer                     01-JUN-83       1000
         2 Ricky Blake                      01-DEC-75        600
         3 Karty Sheen                      06-MAR-85        700

6 rows selected.

SQL>
```

Our test record with employee number **6** can be seen in the preceding screenshot.

# Summary

After completing this chapter, the reader should be able to perform basic Oracle database backups, configure the RMAN environment, change the ARCHIVELOG mode of a database, and recover the database from any media failures.

In this chapter we have used both manual RMAN commands and Oracle-supplied scripts for backup and recovery. At this point, we strongly suggest the reader of this book to refer to Oracle documentation for more details on database backup and recovery.

The next chapter will focus on the performance tuning of the database and database applications. It will cover the best practices in designing efficient database applications and more.

# References

- *Oracle Database Backup and Recovery User's Guide*
  (http://docs.oracle.com/cd/E11882_01/backup.112/e10642/toc.htm)

# 12
# Tuning Oracle Database 11*g* XE

*People with clear, written goals, accomplish far more in a shorter period of time than people without them could ever imagine. - Brian Tracy*

This chapter is dedicated to database tuning. We will discuss various best practices in designing database applications and different techniques of tuning the overall database. The objective of this chapter is to provide a basic foundation in performance tuning. A complete tuning solution is out of the scope of this book. We will briefly discuss the following topics in this chapter:

- Performance tuning
- Performance tuning approach
- Avoiding common pitfalls
- Autotrace utility
- Explain Plan
- Using indexes
- Dynamic performance views
- Statspack

## Performance tuning

**Tuning** is a process of identifying and resolving the cause of slow performing piece of program code. One of the important duties of a database administrator is to ensure that the Oracle database is tuned properly. Tuning is an iterative process. Resolving the first bottleneck may not lead to immediate performance improvement because another bottleneck might be identified which could have bigger a impact on performance.

# Performance tuning approach

Cary Millsap, in his book *Optimizing Oracle Performance*, describes a performance tuning methodology called "Method R". The following are the steps that Method R proposes:

1. Select the user actions for which the business needs improved performance.
2. Collect diagnostic data that will identify the cause of performance degradation.
3. Implement the change and measure the impact. If there is no performance gain then suspend performance improvement activity.
4. Go to step 1.

Performance improvement activity is not only related to the database but could be related to any of these areas—application tuning, operating system tuning, network tuning, I/O tuning, SQL tuning, and database tuning.

# Avoiding common pitfalls

It is commonly considered that performance tuning is a secondary task or a post-production task, but performance tuning should start with the database design phase. Unfortunately, performance tuning is often not considered until there is actually a problem to be fixed.

The following are a few of the commonly misconfigured areas that should be carefully addressed.

# Database connection management

A poor connection management may lead to scalability issues. The applications connect and disconnect very frequently for each database interaction. This is considered bad because establishing a database connection is a resource-expensive task as it involves allocating resources at OS level, negotiating a database connection with Oracle Listener, as well as connecting and allocating memory to database session.

# Cursors and the shared pool

Reusing SQL statements is a key to efficient cursor management. Bind variables should be used whenever possible to avoid hard parsing of SQL statements. To understand bind variables, consider an application that generates hundreds of SELECT statements against a table, as shown next:

```
SQL> SELECT emp_name, salary FROM emp WHERE emp_no = 101;
SQL> SELECT emp_name, salary FROM emp WHERE emp_no = 102;
SQL> SELECT emp_name, salary FROM emp WHERE emp_no = 103;
```

When a SQL query is submitted to an Oracle database, it checks in the shared pool to see whether this statement has already been submitted before. If it has, then the previously submitted statement is retrieved and executed. If the statement is not found in the shared pool, Oracle parses the statement and generates an execution plan. This process is known as a **hard parse**. Instead, write our queries as shown below:

```
SQL> SELECT emp_name, salary FROM emp WHERE emp_no = :p_emp_no;
```

Executing this query hundreds of times will reuse the existing execution plan from the shared pool, thereby avoiding hard parses.

# Suboptimal SQL

A suboptimal SQL uses significant system resources to achieve a task which could have otherwise been achieved using fewer system resources. Read *Analytic Functions: A Savior* on my blog for an example of a suboptimal SQL.

# Incorrect redo log sizing

Often redo log files are left at their default size and with too few online redo log files in production environments. Allocating the right number of redo log files and correctly sizing the redo log files is essential to database performance. If the redo log files are too small in size then the database will spend more time in switching redo log files than doing the real work, and when too few redo log files are allocated then Log Writer Process most likely has to wait for the Archiver process to complete archiving. These waits would then contribute to the degraded performance of the database. Read *Redo Log Switches at their Peak* on my blog for an example of incorrect redo log file sizing.

# Autotrace utility

The autotrace is an SQL*Plus utility used in tuning SQL statements. The autotrace utility offers SQL statement tracing. The PLUSTRACE role is required by the database user enabling trace. The PLUSTRACE role is created by executing the $ORACLE_HOME/sqlplus/admin/plustrce.sql script as SYSDBA.

Tracing is enabled/disabled using the `set autotrace` command in SQL*Plus, shown as follows:

```
SQL> set autotrace on
SQL> set autotrace off
```

The `autotrace` utility does not generate any trace files; instead the trace output is displayed on the screen. The following are the `autotrace` supported options:

- `on`: This enables all options
- `off`: This disables tracing
- `on explain`: This displays returned rows and the execution plan
- `on statistics`: This displays returned rows and statistics
- `trace explain`: This displays the execution plan without actually executing it
- `traceonly`: This displays the execution plan and statistics without returning the rows

The following is an example usage of the `autotrace` utility:

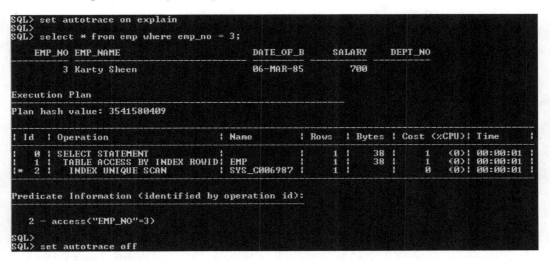

TKPROF is an Oracle database utility used to format SQL trace output into a human readable format.

# Explain Plan

The execution plan of a query is the sequence of operations that Oracle performs to execute a given statement. It is nothing but a tree which contains the order of steps and relationship between them. The Explain Plan statement displays the execution plan chosen by the Oracle Optimizer.

The Explain Plan generates an execution plan and saves it in the PLAN_TABLE. To create a PLAN_TABLE in your schema execute the ORACLE_HOME\rdbms\admin\ utlxplan.sql script.

The following are the basic rules of the execution plan tree:

1.  An execution plan will contain a root, which has no parent.

2.  A parent can have one or more children.

3.  A child has only one parent.

Let us create a dept table in our HR schema, add a foreign key to the emp table pointing to the dept table, and generate an execution plan for an SQL statement joining these two tables. This is done as follows:

```
-- Create DEPT table
SQL> CREATE TABLE dept (dept_no NUMBER(3) PRIMARY KEY, dept_name
VARCHAR2(30));

-- Alter EMP table to add DEPT_NO column & foreign key
SQL> ALTER TABLE emp ADD (dept_no NUMBER(3) REFERENCES dept(dept_no));
```

The following screenshot shows the **EXPLAIN PLAN** command:

```
SQL>
SQL> EXPLAIN PLAN FOR
  2    SELECT e.emp_no, e.emp_name, d.dept_name
  3    FROM emp e, dept d
  4    WHERE e.dept_no = d.dept_no;

Explained.

SQL>
```

The previous command will create an execution plan in the PLAN_TABLE. Run the following **SELECT** statement to retrieve the execution plan in a readable format:

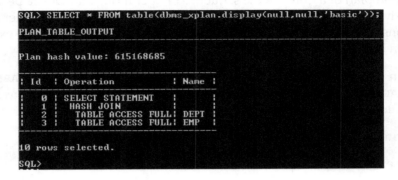

The following is a graphical representation of the execution plan:

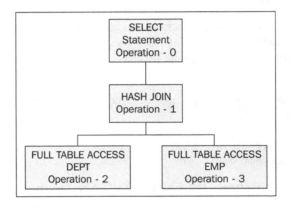

- **Operation – 2** is performed first (a full table access to the DEPT table)
- **Operation – 3** is performed next(a full table access to the EMP table)
- A **HASH JOIN Operation** is performed on the result sets produced by **Operations 2** and **3** (**HASH JOIN Operation**).
- **Operation – 1** returns the results to **Operation – 0**

Another approach of retrieving the actual execution plan is to query the V$SQL_PLAN view. This view was introduced in Oracle 9i and contains the execution plan information.

# Using indexes

Indexes are crucial database objects of your database. Indexes help queries in fetching data using fewer system resources thereby speeding the queries. However, care should be taken when creating new indexes. Too many indexes will lead to negative database performance for DML statements and too few indexes would increase the response time of the queries. Read the *How much expensive are indexes?* post on my blog to understand the impact of having too many indexes for a table.

There are different types of indexes that you may find in Oracle. Below are a few of the index types.

**B*Tree indexes**: These are the most commonly used indexes in the Oracle database. They are named after a computer science construct of the same name. B*Tree indexes provide a faster access to an individual row or range of rows normally requiring few system resources. In a B*Tree, every new table record with a not null indexed column will have an entry in the index. The indexes created earlier in this book are examples of B*Tree indexes.

**Reverse key indexes**: The reverse key indexes are internally implemented as B*Tree indexes. However, the bytes of each index columns are reversed. These indexes are useful for columns which are populated with increasing values. Entries are reversed to distribute the rows more evenly across the index.

For example, if we are using a sequence to generate employee numbers (EMP_NO) in our EMP table with values such as 100, 101, 102, and 103. In a normal B*Tree index these values may go to the same index block, increasing contention for that block. With a reverse key index, these values will be stored as 001, 101, 201, and 301 respectively. This way the values are spread across the index. The following is an example of creating a reverse key index:

```
-- Create reverse key index
SQL>CREATE INDEX emp_rki_idx ON emp(salary) REVERSE;
```

**Function-based Indexes (FBI):**These are special indexes which store the computed result of a function on a rows column(s). Defining a function based index on the transformed column allows that data to be returned using the index when that function is used in the WHERE/ORDER BY clause of a query.

Let us create a function-based index by transforming the emp_name column of the emp table into UPPER case:

```
-- Create function-based index
SQL> CREATE INDEX emp_name_fbi ON emp( UPPER(emp_name) );
```

As the value of UPPER (emp_name) has already been computed and stored in the index, queries of the following form will use this index to fetch the result set faster using fewer resources. The following screenshot demonstrates how queries could benefit from function-based indexes:

```
SQL> set autotrace traceonly exp
SQL>
SQL> select * from emp where UPPER(emp_name) = 'KARTY SHEEN';

Execution Plan
----------------------------------------------------------
Plan hash value: 2797656191

-------------------------------------------------------------------------------------
| Id  | Operation                   | Name        | Rows | Bytes | Cost (%CPU)| Time     |
-------------------------------------------------------------------------------------
|   0 | SELECT STATEMENT            |             |    1 |    26 |     2   (0)| 00:00:01 |
|   1 |  TABLE ACCESS BY INDEX ROWID| EMP         |    1 |    26 |     2   (0)| 00:00:01 |
|*  2 |   INDEX RANGE SCAN          | EMP_NAME_FBI|    1 |       |     1   (0)| 00:00:01 |
-------------------------------------------------------------------------------------

Predicate Information (identified by operation id):
---------------------------------------------------

   2 - access(UPPER("EMP_NAME")='KARTY SHEEN')

SQL>
SQL> set autotrace off
```

# Index monitoring

To maintain optimal database performance drop indexes that your application is not using. Follow these steps to find out whether an index is being used or not:

1.  Enable index monitoring:

    ```
    SQL> ALTER INDEX hr.emp_department_ix MONITORING USAGE;
    ```

2.  Leave the index in monitoring state for a brief period.

3.  Disable index monitoring:

    ```
    SQL> ALTER INDEX emp_department_ix NOMONITORING USAGE;
    ```

4.  Query the V$OBJECT_USAGE view to find out whether the index was used or not:

    ```
    SQL> SELECT monitoring, used
      2  FROM v$object_usage
      3  WHERE index_name = 'EMP_DEPARTMENT_IX';
    ```

5.  Based on the output of USED column, you may decide whether to drop or leave the index. You have to be careful that a particular index may not be used during normal database operations but may be used during monthly/ quarter processing. Make sure that you have chosen a good period to monitor the index.

# Dynamic performance views

Dynamic performance views (V$) are owned by SYS. The dynamic performance views maintained by the Oracle database instance reflect various database metrics since the time when the instance was started. There are three categories of V$ views: current state views, accumulated views, and information views.

The following is a list of a few important V$ views with a short description of each:

- `V$VERSION`: displays database version details
- `V$LOCK`: lists details of currently held locks in the database
- `V$PROCESS`: displays information about currently active processes
- `V$SESSION`: sessions currently connected to the database
- `V$SESSION_EVENT`: provides information about the event that each session is waiting for
- `V$SESSION_WAIT`: displays information about wait events for which active sessions are currently waiting
- `V$SESSTAT`: displays statistics for all the sessions connected to the database
- `V$SQL`: displays statistics on each shared SQL cursor
- `V$SQLTEXT`: displays the actual SQL text for each shared SQL cursor in the SGA
- `V$TRANSACTION`: displays active transactions in the database

# Statspack

The Statspack utility has been available since Oracle 8i (8.1.6) to monitor database performance. Statspack stores the performance statistics in Oracle tables. The data collected can later be used for reporting and performance analysis.

# Installing Statspack

When you run the Statspack installation script, it automatically creates a PERFSTAT user. PERFSTAT owns all the objects needed by the Statspack. The installation steps are as follows:

1. Log into SQL*Plus with the `SYSDBA` privilege.
2. Create a tablespace to hold STATSPACK data (for example, PERFSTAT_TBS).
3. Execute the `spcreate.sql` file which resides in the `ORACLE_HOME/rdbms/admin` folder:

    ```
    -- script to create STATSPACK package
    SQL> @?\rdbms\admin\spcreate.sql
    ```

When the above script is run, it will prompt for the following information:

1. Enter a password for the PERFSTAT user.
2. Choose a tablespace (PERFSTAT_TS).
3. Choose a temporary tablespace.
4. Check the `spcpkg.lis` file for any errors.

If `spcpkg.lis` reports any errors then correct them and rerun the `spcreate.sql` script.

# Gathering statistics

Each collection of statistics is called a **snapshot**. You generate a Statspack report between any two snapshots. The following is the procedure for capturing snapshots:

1. Log in to SQL*Plus as the PERFSTAT user.
2. Execute the `snap` procedure of the STATSPACK package to capture the statistics as follows. When you execute the `snap` procedure, Oracle populates your PERFSTAT tables with the current statistics:

   ```
   SQL> exec statspack.snap;
   ```
3. Run your procedure.
4. Execute the snap procedure of the STATSPACK package as follows:

   ```
   SQL> exec statspack.snap;
   ```

Apart from the preceding manual procedure of capturing the snapshots, we can automate the snapshot capture process using the `spauto.sql` script. I leave this as an exercise for the readers of this book.

# Running the statistics report

You generate statistics report for the period between two snapshots using the `spreport.sql` script located in the `ORACLE_HOME\rdbms\admin` folder as follows:

```
SQL> @?\rdbms\admin\spreport
```

Choose the starting and ending `snap` IDs and optionally choose a name for the STATSPACK report.

# Recommended blogs

I would recommend the readers of this book to religiously follow the following blogs:

- Jonathan Lewis (`http://jonathanlewis.wordpress.com`)
- Tom Kyte (`http://tkyte.blogspot.com`)
- Riyaj Shamsudeen (`http://orainternals.wordpress.com/`)
- Christian Antognini (`http://antognini.ch/blog/`)
- Tanel Poder (`http://blog.tanelpoder.com/`)
- Richard Foote (`http://richardfoote.wordpress.com/`)

They all are very well known Oracle Experts.

# Summary

This chapter has introduced you to the world of performance tuning. Performance tuning is such a huge topic that it requires a book for itself. In this chapter we have learned basic SQL tracing using the `autotrace` utility. When you are requested to investigate a poorly performing SQL statement, you will find Explain Plan to be very helpful and it is one of the starting points in the tuning process. We have also explored different types of indexes in this chapter. STATSPACK reports the overall health of the database. If used correctly it helps solve many of the performance tuning issues related to database memory configuration, I/O configuration, bad performing SQL statements, and so on.

# References

- Oracle Database Performance Tuning Guide 11*g* Release 2
- The Method R tuning methodology is a work of Cary Millsap. For more details I recommend reading his book *Optimizing Oracle Performance*
- *Expert Oracle Database Architecture: Oracle Database 9i, 10g, and 11g Programming Techniques and Solution* by Thomas Kyte
- *Oracle Core: Essential Internals for DBAs and Developers* by Jonathan Lewis
- *Oracle Wait Interface: A Practical Guide to Performance Diagnostics and Tuning* by Gopalakrishnan and Richmond Shee

- *Analytic Functions: A Savior* (`http://momendba.blogspot.com/2008/11/analytic-funcions-savior.html`)

- *Redo Log Switches at their Peak* (`http://momendba.blogspot.com/2011/02/redo-log-switches-at-their-peak.html`)

- *How much expensive are Indexes?* (`http://momendba.blogspot.com/2008/03/how-much-expensive-are-indexes.html`)

- Oracle's whitepaper—*The Oracle Optimizer - Explain the Explain Plan* (`http://www.oracle.com/technetwork/database/focus-areas/bi-datawarehousing/twp-explain-the-explain-plan-052011-393674.pdf`)

# Features Available with Oracle Database 11g XE

This appendix lists all the features that are available with Oracle Database 11g Express Edition.

## Features available

This section lists all the features available in Oracle Database 11g Express Edition. These features are as follows:

- Automatic Datafile Management
- Automatic Memory Management (AMM)
- Automatic Undo Management (AUM)
- Automatic Optimizer Statistics Management
- PL/SQL stored procedures and triggers
- Index Organized Tables (IOT)
- Temporary tables
- External tables
- Large Objects (LOB) support
- Oracle Text
- Native XML support
- Function-based Indexes (FBI)

- SQL Analytical Functions
- Multiple block size support
- Renaming and dropping of column
- Flashback query
- RMAN Online Backup
- Incremental backup and recovery without block change tracking
- Encryption toolkit
- Advanced Queuing

# Features not available

A short list of options and features that are not included with Oracle Database 11g XE:

- Block change tracking
- Flashback database
- Online index rebuild
- Online table redefinition
- Oracle RAC One Node
- Tablespace point-in-time recovery
- Oracle Real Application Clusters (RAC)
- PL/SQL Function Result Cache
- Database resource manager
- Advanced compression
- Oracle Real Application Testing
- Oracle Partitioning

# Index

## Symbols

## A

## B

## C

views
about 44
creating 45
managing 45

# W

workplace 62

# X

XE
about 6, 7
features 7
licensing restrictions 7

## Thank you for buying
# Oracle Database XE 11gR2 Jump Start Guide

## About Packt Publishing

Packt, pronounced 'packed', published its first book "Mastering phpMyAdmin for Effective MySQL Management" in April 2004 and subsequently continued to specialize in publishing highly focused books on specific technologies and solutions.

Our books and publications share the experiences of your fellow IT professionals in adapting and customizing today's systems, applications, and frameworks. Our solution based books give you the knowledge and power to customize the software and technologies you're using to get the job done. Packt books are more specific and less general than the IT books you have seen in the past. Our unique business model allows us to bring you more focused information, giving you more of what you need to know, and less of what you don't.

Packt is a modern, yet unique publishing company, which focuses on producing quality, cutting-edge books for communities of developers, administrators, and newbies alike. For more information, please visit our website: www.packtpub.com.

## About Packt Enterprise

In 2010, Packt launched two new brands, Packt Enterprise and Packt Open Source, in order to continue its focus on specialization. This book is part of the Packt Enterprise brand, home to books published on enterprise software – software created by major vendors, including (but not limited to) IBM, Microsoft and Oracle, often for use in other corporations. Its titles will offer information relevant to a range of users of this software, including administrators, developers, architects, and end users.

## Writing for Packt

We welcome all inquiries from people who are interested in authoring. Book proposals should be sent to author@packtpub.com. If your book idea is still at an early stage and you would like to discuss it first before writing a formal book proposal, contact us; one of our commissioning editors will get in touch with you.

We're not just looking for published authors; if you have strong technical skills but no writing experience, our experienced editors can help you develop a writing career, or simply get some additional reward for your expertise.

## Getting Started with Oracle Data Integrator 11*g*: A Hands-On Tutorial

ISBN: 978-1-84968-068-4        Paperback: 384 pages

Develop and manage robust Java applications with Oracle's high-performance Java Virtual Machine

1.  Discover the comprehensive and sophisticated orchestration of data integration tasks made possible with ODI, including monitoring and error-management

2.  Get to grips with the product architecture and building data integration processes with technologies including Oracle, Microsoft SQL Server and XML files

3.  A comprehensive tutorial packed with tips, images and best practices

## Oracle Database 11*g* – Underground Advice for Database Administrators

ISBN: 978-1-84968-000-4        Paperback: 348 pages

A Practical Guide for developers and architects to the Enterprise Java Beans Standard

1.  A comprehensive handbook aimed at reducing the day-to-day struggle of Oracle 11*g* Database newcomers

2.  Real-world reflections from an experienced DBA—what novice DBAs should really know

3.  Implement Oracle's Maximum Availability Architecture with expert guidance

Please check **www.PacktPub.com** for information on our titles

**OCA Oracle Database 11g: SQL Fundamentals I: A Real-World Certification Guide**

Ace the 1ZO-051 OCA Fundamentals I exam and become a successful DBA by learning how SQL concepts work in the real world

**Steve Ries**

[PACKT] enterprise ⌘

### OCA Oracle Database 11*g*: SQL Fundamentals I: A Real World Certification Guide ( 1ZO-051 )

ISBN: 978-1-84968-364-7            Paperback: 460 pages

Creating, validating, and transforming XML documents with Oracle's IDE

1. Successfully clear the first stepping stone towards attaining the Oracle Certified Associate Certification on Oracle Database 11g

2. This book uses a real world example-driven approach that is easy to understand and makes engaging

3. Complete coverage of the prescribed syllabus

**Business Intelligence: A Project Lifecycle Approach Using Oracle Technology Cookbook**

Over 80 quick and advanced recipes that focus on real world techniques and solutions to manage, design, and build data warehouse and business intelligence projects.

**John Heaton**

[PACKT] enterprise ⌘

### Business Intelligence: A Project Lifecycle Approach Using Oracle Technology Cookbook

ISBN: 978-1-84968-548-1            Paperback: 400  pages

Over 80 quick and advanced recipes that focus on real world techniques and solutions to manage, design, and build data warehouse and business intelligence projects

1. Full of illustrations, diagrams, and tips with clear step-by-step instructions and real time examples to perform key steps and functions on your project

2. Practical ways to estimate the effort of a data warehouse solution based on a standard work breakdown structure

3. Learn to effectively turn the project from development to a live solution

Please check **www.PacktPub.com** for information on our titles

www.ingramcontent.com/pod-product-compliance
Lightning Source LLC
Chambersburg PA
CBHW082121070326
40690CB00049B/4027